M000202095

Pieces Falling absolutely belongs on your bookshelf, but you'll want extra copies in your backpack or glove compartment. The book is more than a beautifully crafted 9/11 memoir; *Pieces Falling* is a tool for sharing hope in the aftermath of any trauma or tragedy. Eschewing victimhood, Ann finds resilience powered by faith, family, and the FDNY. *Pieces Falling* will be in our toolkit on every deployment.

—**Bill and Grace Wiser,** *Rapid Response Team chaplains, Australia*

☙

In *Pieces Falling* Ann Van Hine shares her private journey through an extensively covered public event. On September 11, 2001, Ann's husband, Bruce, responds to the World Trade Center attacks. By midnight he is one of the 343 FDNY firefighters who are unaccounted for. In honest and engrossing prose Ann navigates a personal tragedy which threatens, but never succeeds, in defining her. Instead, she listens for the still small voice of God and discovers an unexpected strength. A triumph to the power of storytelling, this memoir reminds us that to recount our darkest days can be a luminous tribute to life.

—**Donna Kaz,** *author of* Un/Masked: Memoirs of a Guerrilla Girl on Tour *and* Performing Tribute 9/11

Ann and I both share the still unimaginable loss of our firefighter husbands on September 11, 2001. We also both have a very deep faith in God, which keeps us going. In *Pieces Falling*, you will read how this deep faith, love of family and friends brought her through this darkness and sorrow. She expresses so eloquently that with God's good grace one can go through tragedy and sorrow and still believe that life is good and beautiful.

—*JoAnn Atlas, FDNY widow*

❧

From the opening words of "I'm blessed!" to "See you later," every word of this story is readable and captivating. It is not a story about 9/11—it is the story of Bruce and Ann, their love, their family, their faith. It's the story of all the days before and after, with September 11 being the bridge. It will make you smile, make you laugh, make you cry, sometimes all within the same page. But by the end, you will know Ann, Meghan, Emily, and NY Firefighter Richard "Bruce" Van Hine. You will know their story. You will have journeyed through a marriage and kids, holidays and a "new normal," the FDNY, and faith in God. And to that Bruce would say, "I'm blessed I'm married to Miss Ann, and I have the best girls in the world."

—***Rev. Bruce Barnard,*** *president and executive director of the Manhattan Initiative and director of operations and finance for the Metro New York District for the Church of the Nazarene*

Pieces Falling is an incredible story of Ann Van Hine's journey through the loss of her husband, Bruce, who died in the line of duty on September 11, 2001. Ann shares her experiences of events, 'tricky days,' and how life continued through celebrations and grieving. Ann takes us from giggles to tears and the Godly response to life-changing events. She helps us see the events in life don't define us. We can define them. God is with us through it all. May we all glean from the wisdom provided in *Pieces Falling*.

—**Billie Jauss,** *speaker, and author of* Making Room: Doing Less So God Can Do More. *www.billiejauss.com*

ॐ

Ann shares her unique heartfelt journey finding strength, patience, and grace to embrace a new mosaic of life while honoring her husband. She keeps a beacon of light shining throughout the journey in her faith which enables her to open her heart to be present and mindful of her choices. Her humility brings an honest humor to the presence of circumstances most of us could never imagine. Reading her story enriches your soul and your faith in humanity.

—**Jenunifer Adams-Webb,** *CEO and Co-Founder 9/11 Tribute Museum and the September 11*[th] *Families Association*

The event of 9/11 is not over...it continues in many ways including in powerful stories of lives altered by that tragic day. In *Pieces Falling*, Ann Van Hine shares her moving story of 9/11's impact on her life and family as a way to empower all of us to come closer to understanding what happened and to offer lessons of resilience. Ann has graciously shared her story with people from New York to Japan and we all owe her a debt of gratitude to putting it writing for a larger audience.

*—**David P. Janes,** Senior Advisor to the President for Institutional Development Okinawa Institute of Science and Technology Graduate University (OIST) Chair of the Board and Co-Founder EngageAsia*

ॐ

An incredible story of faith, the care of a loving family, friends, and community as the courageous family of an FDNY hero walks through the tricky days between devastating loss and a new normal. *Pieces Falling* records in written form Ann Van Hine's story that has inspired so many in the twenty years since 9/11.

*—**Tom Dykhouse,** Executive Director & Head of School, Eastern Christian School Association*

Grab your tissues and get ready to build your faith as you read through Ann Van Hine's *Pieces Falling*. In this true story, Ann Van Hine unveils her faith journey as the wife of a fallen fire fighter who lost his life as one of the heroes of September 11. You don't have to be a fire fighter's spouse or family member to be moved by this book. It may feel as if you are signing up to be sad by diving into these pages, but in truth, you will leave this story changed and with greater faith. This reminder of how our Comforter works in the big and small details left me feeling encouraged and wanting pass along encouragement to others.

—*Shontell Brewer, Author of* Missionary Mom,
Wife to Mike Brewer, Fire Captain in Reno, Nevada

૭

Pieces Falling is a profoundly moving account of one woman's story of rebuilding her life after the loss of her FDNY husband on 9/11. Ann is a gifted storyteller and an observant writer with a keen sense of capturing dialogue, particularly of her two wise children. While Ann's Christian faith is her bedrock, this book will appeal to people of all faiths: Because at its core, *Pieces Falling* is an intricate portrait of how family, friends and community came together in myriad ways to support and lift up Ann and continue to do so twenty years after that terrible day.

—*Scott Elliott, Filmmaker & director 590films*

Most 9/11 stories are intense and sensational, about the horrific events of the day everyone in America remembers. But this one is different; this is a beautiful tribute not to a victim, but to an American hero. With the encouragement of his beloved wife Ann, Bruce Van Hine chased his childhood dream of becoming a New York City firefighter. His dream came true but then he was lost in the World Trade Center attacks, leaving Ann and his girls behind. This is not just the story of an unforgettable tragedy; it's a love story, a loss story, a grief story, and a hero's story. Bruce was the best kind of hero—a kind, strong, and courageous man who chose a dangerous job to serve others. In her book, *Pieces Falling*, Ann pieces together his legacy, which becomes her own as she begins to tell her story and serve others in a different way than Bruce did, as she becomes a keeper of a powerful story, continuing a legacy of service.

—**Susy Flory**, *New York Times bestselling author and co-author, and director of West Coast Christian Writers*

ॐ

I often have moments in life when I ask God, "where are you in the midst of such sadness?" God has yet to provide me with a direct answer. There's no booming voice with a clear explanation. And yet, Ann Van Hine's story provides glimpses of God's steadfast love and presence, even in the midst of tremendous pain and loss. *Pieces Falling* has become my go-to book for what faith can look like in the real world.

—**Rev. Ann Kansfield**, *FDNY chaplain*

We all have a 9/11 story. We remember where we were when we first heard the news. Each story is unique, yet we are all tethered together in this tragedy of international scope. *Pieces Falling* tells one story, but in it, author Ann Van Hine provides universal insights that serve to build our faith in God and in humanity. Her words of wisdom will live on to teach and encourage me and all her readers for years to come. My faith is stronger for having known Ann and having read her story. Yours will be too.

—*Susan Panzica, Speaker : Writer : Abolitionist*

PIECES
FALLING

PIECES
FALLING

Navigating 9/11 with Faith, Family and the FDNY

One woman's journey

ANN VAN HINE

MEDIA.COM

PIECES
FALLING

I strived to present a truthful account, but memory, like time, is a strange thing. This is how I remember the events described. Conversations have been recreated and maybe even supplemented to move the story forward. A few names have been changed to protect privacy. And a few names are probably mixed up—my apologies. The word *brotherhood* is used regarding the FDNY because, to be honest, I couldn't find another word that fit that kind of camaraderie. It isn't gender specific.

The views and opinions expressed in this book are those of the author and do not necessarily reflect the official policy or position of Illumify Media Global.

Published by
Illumify Media Global
www.IllumifyMedia.com
"We bring your book to life!"

Library of Congress Control Number: 2021911325

Paperback ISBN: 978-1-955043-22-9
eBook ISBN: 978-1-955043-23-6

Typeset by Art Innovations (http://artinnovations.in/)
Cover design by Debbie Lewis

Printed in the United States of America

"We will not hide these truths from our children; we will tell the next generation about the glorious deeds of the Lord, about his power and his mighty wonders."

Psalm 78:4 NLT

CONTENTS

ACKNOWLEDGEMENTS

∞

As I say on walking tours, we don't do life alone. And that applies to writing a book, especially when you are new to writing.

Thank you to all the faculty and staff at the Mount Hermon Writers Conference for the opportunities to explore the world of writing. Shout outs to Jan Kern for your instruction during the preconference and mentor programs, to Susy Flory for your kindness and encouragement, and to Susan King for suggesting I submit a devotional to *The Upper Room*. And thank you, Joan Ball, for suggesting I go to Mount Hermon Writers Conference as my first baby step into this new world.

Thank you to Illumify Media. So glad our paths crossed at the Philadelphia Writers Conference. Karen Bouchard, my book coach extraordinaire, your expertise, patience, and encouragement are a blessing. I smile every time I think of you saying, "Give me a moment as I read ahead." Then silence followed by "Where is this going?" Good question. Thanks for helping me write the answer.

Thank you to the North Jersey Christian Writers Group. I wasn't with you often, but those occasions were invaluable. Thank you, Barbara H., Susan P., and so many others.

In a world of virtual assistants, I was blessed to have a real one. Thank you, Liz B.

"Don't walk ahead of me; I may not follow. Don't walk behind me; I may not lead. Just walk beside me and be my friend." Albert Camus

I have been blessed with many amazing friends. Each of our friendships enriches my life.

Carol: my person. Thank you for being you.

Debbie, JoEllen, Sue, Kathy, Julie, Diane, Linda, Jen, Joanne, Pat, Jane: Thank you for your prayers and for numerous memories of doing life together through many years.

Steve and Karen and Bruce and Amy: thank you for being my pastors and friends.

Doug and Rene: thank you for never making me feel like a third wheel (and never letting me get a big head).

9/11 Tribute Museum docents and staff: Thank you for the opportunities you have given me to share my story and learn yours.

TLA: our weekly Zooms have sustained me during the pandemic. Thank you. Here's to more adventures *being tourists in our own city.*

To my family: thank you for being there through the mountains, the valleys, and the plains of life. Once it is safe to travel, I am heading in your direction.

To my girls and their guys: I love you. I am so very proud of you.

To Bruce: I cherish the life we shared. I miss you. I love you. I will see you later.

FOREWORD

BY FDNY CAPTAIN (RETIRED) BRENDA BERKMAN,
9/11 FIRST RESPONDER

When Googling "September 11, 2001," you can find this summary on Britannica.com: "a series of airline hijackings and suicide attacks committed in 2001 by 19 terrorists associated with the Islamic extremist group al-Qaeda. It was the deadliest terrorist attack on U.S. soil; nearly 3,000 people were killed." Searching "books about September 11, 2001" brings up 477,000,000 results. You could spend a lot of years reading Wikipedia's partial list of 9/11-themed books.

So why read *Pieces Falling* and why read it now, twenty years after September 11? A different and important perspective is added to the mosaic of 9/11 historical narratives as Ann tells her story—the story of an FDNY widow of strong Christian faith left to raise two young daughters. Much about Ann's story is not a universal story. Unlike most families suffering the death of a loved one, hers had to go through the loss of their firefighter husband and father Bruce in the glare of international attention.

After 9/11, the focus of the media—and hence the public's attention—was on the 343 lost New York City firefighters.

Perhaps more than any other group, the firefighters' deaths had to have meaning—to stand for something—so their loss would not have been in vain. The media and the public demanded that. The intense focus on the firefighters' families thrust Ann and others into the spotlight—people who had no experience dealing with that "celebrity" experience. New York City as the epicenter of media at the time only increased the intensity of that attention and hypersensitivity to every word and action related to 9/11. Every anniversary of the attack on the World Trade Center is a revisiting of the loss. A family tragedy is not usually part of a paradigm–shifting historical loss.

But much of Ann's story is universal, that of what happens when one parent dies and the remaining parent is left to pick up the pieces. As Ann recounts the seemingly mundane details of her life after the loss of Bruce—rearranging the furniture at home, buying a new car—we experience her step–by–step path to coping with a sudden and deep loss. Ann was determined that her family's life would be defined not by loss but resilience and hope as she created a "new normal" for herself and her teenage daughters post-9/11. With inspiration and support from her Christian faith community, Ann rose to the challenges and pressures, relying on God's direction to choose the right actions and speak the right words. Eventually, she sought out ways to tell her story to help others deal with challenges and loss in their own lives.

Ann embodied the wisdom of Maya Angelou who said: "I've learned that whenever I decide something with an open heart, I usually make the right decision." And as the pandemic–traumatized world looks for ways to heal, Ann's story provides many guideposts and, most importantly, hope for the way forward.

WINTER 1980

∞

Bruce sat on an orange vinyl chair at the chrome and Formica kitchen table in our small apartment looking through the classified ads. We were newly married and both small business owners. I owned a dance school, offering ballet, tap, and jazz classes for children and adults. He owned a tree company. But his work of pruning, removing, and feeding trees was definitely seasonal work, leaving him looking for odd jobs through part of the year.

Bruce circled an ad for a taxi driver and took a sip of his coffee.

I admired his work ethic, but his "career of the week" as I called it was exhausting for both of us—and our budget!

Studying my husband, I asked, "What did you always want to be when you grew up?"

"A firefighter, a real firefighter."

"What is a real firefighter?"

"A New York City firefighter!"

"Then go do that."

1

BLESSED

∞

Golden shafts of afternoon sunlight filtered through the windows. I felt the mattress shift as Bruce got out of bed. *Nap time can't be over yet,* I thought. I rolled over and heard his voice.

"I am so blessed."

I opened my eyes and replied, "Why?"

He reached for his Squad 41 polo shirt. "I'm married to Miss Ann."

I chuckled, grabbed the edge of the sheet, and sat up. "Some people wouldn't consider that a perk."

He smiled. "And we have two great kids."

1

"That's true."

Our daughters were born three years and three days apart. No planning, just happened that way. Emily, our seventeen–year–old reserved, attentive child had just started her senior year of high school and had negotiated her schedule to allow for early dismissal. We had informed her that early dismissal required her to volunteer somewhere or get a part–time job. Emily was investigating her options. Volunteering with the Red Cross was top on the list.

At fourteen, Meghan was almost as tall as I was at five feet, ten inches. Meghan was our second born and polar opposite of her older sister. Weeks earlier, after freshman orientation, Meghan had declared, "By the time I have been at high school a month, everyone will know who I am. I kept asking if anyone knew Emily, and no one did. They are going to know me."

I didn't doubt that for a moment.

Bruce sat on the edge of the bed to put his shoes on,

"And we got the trailer. We had a great summer."

"Yes, we did."

After years of tent and pop–up camping, the trailer was a welcome step up. The weeks of summer had flown by with a trip to Indianapolis, volunteering at kids' camp, and attending family camp. In addition, the girls had volunteered to stay and help for an extra week after teen camp, giving Bruce and me a week of "just us" time. It was a wonderful taste of what the future would be like.

He gave me a quick kiss on the cheek and left for the firehouse. He was working a "24," which meant he would work Sunday night to Monday night and then make up a tour on Tuesday. He planned on spending Monday night at the firehouse as it meant less driving. After all, why come home to sleep and then head back in?

THE ATTACK

First there is the attack.

The attack sets your life spiraling in a direction you never expected. It can come in many forms: a diagnosis, an accident, words spoken in haste, a job lost, betrayal, death of a loved one. It can even come from an act of terrorism.

September 11, 2001 attack on New York City:

8:46 a.m. – American Airlines flight 11 flown into 1 WTC.

9:03 a.m. – United Airlines flight 175 flown into 2 WTC.

9:29 a.m. – FDNY issues total recall.

9:59 a.m. – 2 WTC collapses.

10:28 a.m. – 1 WTC collapses.

2

MY FREE DAY

∞

TUESDAY, SEPTEMBER 11

It was supposed to be a get–a–few–things–done type of day. With the girls back in school, Bruce on duty, and one more week until fall classes resumed at my dance studio, I was free to do as I pleased. As a mom, wife, small business owner, and church volunteer, I prided myself on being organized, prepared, in control of my life. "No surprises" was my motto—or perhaps it was my plea to the universe.

The day started as most days did. Wanting to ease into my day instead of being thrown into it, I got up an hour before my daughters to shower, let the dog out, get my thoughts together, and have my cup of tea.

At 6:30 a.m., Meghan staggered into the kitchen, arms at her sides, head down, still half-asleep, and stood in front of me for her morning hug and kiss on the forehead.

Emily walked in moments later. "Mom, don't forget I have that Red Cross meeting this evening. After school, are we coming home before going to the meeting?"

"Probably not. We'll run errands or visit Nanny and Poppy"

Meghan chimed in. "What's happening to me?"

"Still sorting that out. Daddy will probably bring you home. Let's go, girls."

The target time to leave the house each school day was 7:15 a.m. My daughters attended a small Christian high school in North Haledon, thirty miles away across the border in New Jersey. Even though their school was miles from home, it was near to my studio, making me available for drop-offs, pick-ups, and emergencies during the day.

Forty-five minutes later as I turned into the circular driveway of the girls' school, I commented, "Make sure you have all of your stuff. Em, I'll see you at early dismissal time. Meg, I'll see you at regular time. Have a good day. Love you."

Next, I headed to my dance studio to quickly check the mail and answering machine messages before heading home for my uncharacteristically free morning.

Can't wait!

I had just gotten in my car when the radio came on.

"A small plane has flown into the World Trade Center."

As I put the car into reverse, looked over my shoulder and backed up, the radio news anchor continued. "A second plane has hit the World Trade Center."

What? I pulled back into the parking space and sat a moment. I turned up the volume.

I hadn't misheard.

The World Trade Center was under some kind of attack.

I needed to get home. As I merged onto Route 208, the FDNY came on with an announcement.

"All firefighters report for duty."

I knew the FDNY doesn't call firefighters into work via radio announcements! This was bad, really bad.

We must be at war, but with whom?

I was driving on autopilot, barely seeing the road in front of me.

The radio droned on. I started to pray. Lord, protect Bruce. Bring him home.

I knew he would be sent down there.

Bruce was a firefighter in a Special Operations Command (SOC) unit, a Squad. Squad 41 to be exact. Squad 41 ventured into Manhattan from the Bronx on a regular basis. I've joked that firefighters in Squads (and Rescues) do things they don't tell their wives. It is bad enough that your firefighter husband runs into burning buildings. You don't want to know he hung from a building, crawled around in a confined space, or suffered exposure to a biohazard all in the name of an average day in a Squad or Rescue Unit.

When I arrived home, I threw my purse on the chair, grabbed the remote, plopped down on the couch, and turned on the television.

The images of a plane crashing into the Pentagon filled the screen.

The news professionals appeared as shocked and rattled as I was. The images were baffling, as were the reports out of Washington, DC.

Lord, please protect my country. Please protect New York City.

I paced, pleaded, and prayed as the television kept reporting additional events. One of the twin towers collapsed; another plane crashed in Pennsylvania; the other tower collapsed.

I remembered in the Old Testament how Abraham prayed for a city to be saved. He asked God to save the city if even one hundred righteous people could be found. He worked his way down to ten people, and eventually to just one person. I figured I had no time to waste so I begged God to save my city for even just one righteous person. I suggested to God that Dr. Mucci, District Superintendent for the Church of Nazarene, would probably qualify as the one person.

Worried that my brother or brother-in-law might be in the city or flying for business, I tried to make several calls to my parents in New Jersey and sister in New York. No calls would go through.

"All circuits are busy, please try again later."

Suddenly my house phone rang.

"Mom, where is Daddy?" It was Emily.

"I don't know." *I must hold it together until Bruce is home.* "I don't expect to hear from Daddy. He doesn't usually call when he is on duty. We'll call the firehouse later if we haven't heard from him by the time he is off duty. Okay? Find your sister and I'll pick you both up at early release time at two o clock. I love you. See you in a little while."

People have asked me why I didn't get my girls from school when I first heard about the attacks. To be honest, it never dawned on me to get them from school. I think I believed that if the girls were at school, Bruce was on duty, and I was at my dance studio or home, it was all normal. And I desperately needed for it to be normal. For it to be all right.

The phone rang again.

"Hi, it's Barbara. Is Bruce on duty?"

It was my sister, who I hadn't spoken to in a very long time. She lived in California, so I was surprised she had heard about a fire in New York City. I was grateful to hear her voice, even if most of my family and friends knew my house rule: If you hear about a fire on the media, *don't* call me and ask if Bruce is on duty.

After we hung up, my thoughts of having a free day to do as I pleased were forgotten. I wasn't sure what I should do. The television didn't seem to have any new information. The circuits were still overwhelmed so I couldn't make phone calls. As much as I had wanted to hurry home, being home now felt isolating.

I couldn't wait to pick up Emily and Meghan, but it wasn't two o clock yet.

I decided to drive back to the studio to see Carol, my best friend and business partner. She is "my person." We can talk for hours or sit with a cup of tea and not say a word. Through life's mountains and valleys, she's walked with me. We double-dated in our teens and twenties. We stood up for each other when we got married.

When I started my business, New School of Dance Arts, Carol taught for me. After the first year, I asked her if she wanted to be my business partner. At the time, I had $100 in the studio bank account. I told her if she matched the $100, we would be equal partners in the business.

Her hubby, Tony, calls us "partners in crime." Tony and many others chuckled at our lack of business savvy, telling us, "That's not how you buy into a business," but Carol and I have been business partners since 1976 so I guess we've done something right.

I retraced the same route I had driven earlier. But this time, as I approached the top of Skyline Drive, I noticed there were cars parked on the shoulder of the road. People were standing outside their cars.

What are they doing? I wondered.

As the road reached the crest of the mountain, my question was answered. The New York City skyline came into view. Looking to the right, you can usually see Lower Manhattan.

Instead, there was a big cloud of smoke where the buildings had been.

Had I seen the towers when I drove the girls to school? I couldn't remember.

I entered the studio to find Carol sitting at a table with brochures, registration forms, and schedules arranged in front of her.

"Your dad has been calling," were the first words out of her mouth. "He wants you to call him."

I put my purse on the gymnastic mats and reached for the wall phone. A brief conversation with my dad ended with a promise to stop by after I had picked up the girls.

Carol and I discussed all that we knew about the attacks. We switched gears to focus on studio stuff, what classes we needed to confirm, cancel, and so on.

"I will call you when I hear from Bruce," I promised as I walked out the door.

I had no idea it would be three weeks before I would step foot in my studio again.

Over the last three years, I had regularly dropped Emily off or picked her up at school but rarely entered the building. I had been very involved as a teacher or aide during Emily's preschool, elementary school, and junior high years. So, when she started high school, I decided to step back and allow her to be her own person without being known as "Miss Ann's daughter."

But today the whole world felt different. I went into the front office.

"Hi, I am Ann Van Hine. Emily has early release. I also want to sign out Meghan."

"Of course," the woman at the desk responded. "Let me see what class Meghan is in. Emily should be heading this way to sign out."

On the drive to my parents' house, the girls were full of questions. I had no answers, only assurances of love and faith. We arrived at my parents' home nine miles away to find my dad sitting at the far side of the dining room table. Much to my mom's dismay, he had turned it into his desk, so he was surrounded by books and papers. But he wasn't working. He was sitting quietly, waiting for us with a somber look on his face. My mom was still at work.

We joined him at the table.

As we talked, he tried to reassure the girls and me.

"I'm sure your dad is safe. He couldn't have gotten from the Bronx to Lower Manhattan before the towers collapsed."

"But Poppy," one of the girls asked, "how can you be sure?"

"Think about how long takes to get from the Bronx to Lower Manhattan."

My dad is an engineer and physicist so thinking things through logically is a strength of his. But even as he explained his reasoning, I knew he was wrong. He wasn't tuning into the fact that Bruce, in a Squad, would have been dispatched earlier rather than later.

Emily and I discussed the Red Cross meeting. She called the leader and found out it had been cancelled. We hung out a little longer, then decided to head home.

As I drove up Route 17, in my rearview mirror for a brief moment I saw the New York City skyline. I saw the smoke, and mentally, I willed my girls not to turn around. When we got home, we turned the television on for a short time. We tried to do our daily routine. Time slowed or stopped or something— but was definitely not moving as in a normal day.

By the late afternoon, I spoke with my sister-in-law, Bobbie, Bruce's sister. She was visiting at my mother-in-law's home in South Jersey about three hours away, in town for a friend's wedding. My father-in-law had died ten years prior, and my mother-in-law lived alone, and one of my greatest fears had been having to tell her one day that something had happened to her son. I was so relieved that, on September 11, 2001, my eighty-two-year-old mother-in-law was not alone, that Bobbie was with her on that day. *Thank you, Lord.*

Around 7:00 p.m., I went into my bedroom to call Squad 41. The answering machine picked up. I left a message: "Please have Bruce Van Hine call his wife."

I didn't wait long before I called again and left another message: "Please have anyone call Bruce Van Hine's wife."

I called my folks. I told my dad that no one was answering the phone at Squad 41. When my ever-calm dad said, "Call every number you have for the New York City Fire Department until you reach a human being," I was freaked.

Deep breath. I walked quickly down the hall past Meghan's bedroom, peeked my head in, and saw both girls sitting on the bed. I smiled.

"You guys need anything?"

"No, we're good," replied Emily.

I grabbed the FDNY phone list off the back of the basement door and then headed to my bedroom out of earshot of my girls. I glanced down at the list, saw the word Bronx, and dialed.

"Bronx Dispatch."

"My husband is a firefighter with Squad 41. I've called there several times. They aren't answering their phone."

"Ma'am, this is the number to report a fire."

"Oh, sorry."

"Not a problem. Just keep calling them."

"Okay, thank you."

Eventually I got through to someone at Squad 41 who said, "I'm the only one here. Everyone else went to look for them. Someone will be in touch when they get back."

Around 10:00 p.m. I decided we should all get some sleep, so Emily, Meghan and our 130–pound Rottweiler, Buster Brown, piled into my bed. I had a feeling someone might be coming to the house and didn't want to be in my pajamas, so I stayed dressed.

I lay with my girls until they were asleep.

Then I got up.

I paced, prayed, and made a cup of tea. Growing up, a "cup of tea" had always been the quick fix for whatever was happening. A cup of tea could calm you down or cheer you up. My mom is British so making tea was a ritual.

I followed that ritual as I boiled water, heated the pot, steeped the tea, and placed the tea cozy over the pot. I poured the milk in the cup first, added one sugar, and poured the brewed tea.

I sat on the couch cradling my warm cup of tea in my hands and waited. For what I didn't know.

But I waited.

A little before midnight, I heard a car pull up. A car door closed and then another.

Even though the streetlight would have allowed me a glimpse of who was heading to my house if I had chosen to get up and peek through one of the three small windows in my front door, I decided I didn't want to know.

I held my breath and sat perfectly still. *Maybe they aren't coming here. Please don't be coming here.*

There was a light knock on the side door. It dawned on me that whoever it was, they knew us well enough to use the side kitchen instead of the front door.

I walked slowly to the door and opened it.

Standing outside were two men. Charlie was Bruce's lieutenant, hiking partner, and friend. Standing next to Charlie was another firefighter whose name escaped me.

I waved them inside.

While they stood in the kitchen, I backed up and leaned my shoulder against the door frame between the kitchen and living room. The doorway felt solid, strong enough to hold me up if need be.

We exchanged polite greetings.

And then silence.

I couldn't stand the suspense. "Just say it."

Charlie whispered, "They are unaccounted for."

In an almost out–of–body experience I heard myself say, "I have no doubt God can get me through this, but I don't *want* to go through this."

I don't want to. How many times through the years had my kids and my students said those exact same words? How many times had I patiently explained that "most of life has nothing to do with what you *want* to do; I don't *want* to pay taxes or do laundry, but I do it anyway."

I don't remember feeling a sense of dread, just an awareness that this was really happening.

The three of us sat at the kitchen table as Charlie filled me in on what they knew, which wasn't much. Charlie offered assistance, a prayer, a hug, and they left.

I locked the door and tiptoed down the hallway toward my bedroom. I hoped and prayed that the girls were asleep and hadn't heard the exchange with Charlie. When I cracked the door and peeked into the room, they seemed to be asleep, so I went back into the kitchen to make a few calls.

I called Debbie, one of my best friends and also a pastor. I asked her to contact Pastor Steve and other friends in the morning.

As we spoke, I glanced out the window and noticed a man walking down the street. It reminded me of a scene from a movie—the late hour, the single streetlight glowing. It felt eerie. I mentioned it to Debbie. Years later, she reminded me of the guy walking down the street and added, "Maybe it was Bruce checking on things."

After I hung up the phone from talking with Debbie, I called my parents and shared what I knew.

"We'll drive up," my mom said.

"No, it's too late. Come tomorrow. I'm okay. Love you."

I checked on my daughters again and realized Emily was awake. I put my finger to my lips, then gestured for her to follow me. We sat on the living room floor. Within moments Meghan and the dog appeared in the doorway. They joined us on the floor.

"Charlie was here," I told them. "Daddy is unaccounted for."

We cried.

We hugged.

We prayed.

We got back in bed.

Once the girls were asleep, I got up again. I made another pot of tea.

A fragment of a verse kept running through my head: "Sorrow lasts for a night but joy cometh in the morning." I needed to see the sun rise. I waited for the new day. I waited for the darkness to be replaced by the light. I waited until the sun rose, and then I lay down to sleep.

3

JOY COMES IN THE MORNING

∞

WEDNESDAY, SEPTEMBER 12

This was role reversal. Christine, my baby sister, coming to help me. As her big sister by almost thirteen years, I had changed her diaper, taken her to Disney World, driven her to school, been her ballet teacher.

When she was in high school, I was her employer. She graduated from high school just weeks after Emily was born. Through college she had continued to teach for me. Law school ended our employee/employer connection.

At times our relationship had been more mother-daughter than sisters, but here she was standing in my kitchen with her suitcase in hand stating, "I have come to do all those things you can't do and to stay for as long as you need me."

I knew without a doubt there were things she could do that I couldn't—navigate the legal system, ask the right questions, identify a body.

As I hoisted myself up to sit on the kitchen counter, I asked, "But how? Don't you have any cases?" After a brief stint as a corporate lawyer, Christine had become an assistant district attorney.

She sat down at the table. "It's weird. I don't have any cases. Everyone pled guilty." Confused and not sure if she was lying, I was grateful.

My daughters and Christine had a great relationship, so my sister's presence was not only a blessing to me, but it gave me confidence that my girls were in good hands. To see Meghan and Christine greet each other with their elaborate combination dance/handshake created a sense of normality on a day very little was known.

With school canceled, Emily and Meghan didn't have to be anywhere, so the four of us hung out waiting for updates, waiting for the other shoe to drop, waiting to know what to do next.

The very little we knew—"he is unaccounted"—was told and retold as family, friends, and acquaintances called, showed up on my doorstep, or emailed.

Every time the phone rang, I held my breath as I lifted the receiver. Would it be Bruce's voice on the other end?

Throughout the day the television was turned on to glean information. Real information, a much–needed commodity, was hard to find. The television news seemed to broadcast stories without verification. I don't fault the media for that because the need for information was frantic. It was a rollercoaster that wasn't beneficial, so the television was off more than it was on.

By mid-morning I called Squad 41 to see if there was any word. A young firefighter answered the phone. I smiled as he commented that he was all alone and didn't know anything.

I could imagine his fellow firefighters telling him to stay there at the firehouse and answer the phone but offering no other guidance to a newbie who had no clue.

I requested setting up a schedule that Squad 41 would call us, the wives of the unaccounted, twice a day whether there was anything to report or not. He thought that a good idea and promised to pass it along.

Firefighters showed up on my doorstep. The fire department, whether FDNY, West Point, or Greenwood Lake, were fulfilling their promise to care for the families. Firefighters, many covered in ash, looking exhausted, offered bagels, cold cuts, assistance in whatever form I requested. Many spoke of voids—areas of space where they expected to find survivors—as a way of offering assurance.

From that first night when "joy comes in the morning" kept running in my head, I knew God was the only sure thing. I sought guidance from the Bible, and each time God gave me what I needed and more than I expected.

I wasn't doing any intense Bible study. Since my ability to concentrate was gone, I was only looking up verses I knew. I didn't trust myself to remember even the simplest verses correctly, so I read them slowly and deliberately.

A well-known verse in our home was "Finally, brothers, whatever is true, whatever is noble, whatever is right, whatever is pure, whatever is lovely, whatever is admirable—if anything is excellent or praiseworthy—think about such things" (Philippians 4:8 NIV). Many times, Emily and Meghan had heard me quote this as a qualifier. Does the movie you want to see, the thing you want to do pass the test? Is it true, is it right, pure, and admirable?

On Thursday, September 13, as I looked up that verse, my eyes drifted up the page to the verses above. As I read Philippians 4:4–7, it was as if God had written those words for me for this moment. "Rejoice in the Lord always. I will say it again: Rejoice!" There was no stipulation, you don't have to rejoice if your husband is lying at the bottom of the World Trade Center. There was just *Rejoice!* "Let your gentleness be evident to all. The Lord is near." The Lord is near. He is near to me and my girls and Bruce. "Do not be anxious for anything, but in everything, by prayer and petition, with thanksgiving, present your requests to God. And the peace of God, which transcends all understanding, will guard your hearts and minds in Christ Jesus."

Do not be anxious for anything—God has got this. He is in control. He promises His peace. My heart won't be totally broken, and I won't lose my mind because God will guard my heart and mind. *Thank you. Thank you.*

As I reread the "whatever" verses I noticed another promise: "And the God of peace will be with you." I marked the date in the Bible Bruce had given me for Christmas in 1992.

Each time I looked up a familiar verse God showed me something new. "But those who hope in the Lord will renew their strength. They will soar on wings like eagles; they will run and not grow weary, they will walk and not be faint" (Isaiah 40:31).

Look across the center margin: "So do not fear, for I am with you; do not be dismayed, for I am your God. I will strengthen you and help you; I will uphold you with my righteous right hand" (Isaiah 41:10) dated 9/14/01.

Each morning or evening as I read verses, I would leave the Bible open on the end table in the living room to remind me and all who entered of God's promise for that day.

On Thursday, Emily and Meghan chose to go to school, so Christine drove them there. I decided to drive the girls on Friday. I needed to do something normal. I needed to get out of the house. I commented to friends I had spent more time at home in the last few days than I had in months.

On the way home, I stopped at CVS. That was a weird experience. My ability to remember what I needed and where items were located in the store was definitely impaired.

A sense of being in a bubble—separate from my surroundings, almost invisible but completely exposed at the same time—overwhelmed me. How can these people be going about their lives like everything is normal?

I felt there was a big flashing sign on my head: *My husband is missing. May Day. Help.*

I also stopped by my local library. The librarian had a confused look on her face as she looked up from the desk.

"What are you doing here?" she asked.

"My library book is due!"

"Oh, how are you doing?"

"I'm doing!"

"I'm doing" became my pat response to "How are you doing?" I was doing something like returning my book to the library, but as far as how are YOU doing, that question I couldn't answer.

To be honest I didn't know how I was doing; I felt numb but aware of every little thing. Was there a scale or benchmarks that defined how I was doing? I didn't know.

How are you coping? was another question asked time and again. That question was easier to answer because I wasn't coping, I was hoping in God's promises. The words of the Edward Mote hymn went through my head. "My hope is built on nothing less than Jesus' blood and righteousness on Christ the solid rock I stand."

My hope wasn't built on Bruce coming home, which was my heart's desire, but it was built on God is in control.

At first, I said I was hiding behind God and peeking out every now and then to see if it was safe. I envisioned God as this big rock with Emily, Meghan and me crouching securely behind him.

After a while, God became the arms I rested in as He carried me and my girls down a path we never expected to be on.

I was reminded of something that happened at family camp just weeks earlier. Justin, Bruce's godson, was a preschooler at the time. Justin was warned if he kept misbehaving, he'd have to go back to his campsite. Well, he misbehaved again, and his Dad scooped him into his arms to carry him back.

Justin cried and fought against his dad, but all his fussing made little difference. His dad followed through on his promised consequences of not listening: Justin returning to their campsite.

As I remembered that, I was struck by the thought Justin could have rested in his father's arms. Because either way, fussing or resting, he *was* going back to their campsite.

I had the same choice, not because there was disobedience but because this was happening, and I could rest in my Heavenly Father's arms or go kicking and screaming. Either way, it was happening. God eventually put us down to walk, but He was ever ready to scoop us up when we needed the extra support.

In the first days after the attacks, I was amazed by the outpouring of encouragement from friends, family, and strangers—the telephone constantly rang, people arrived with food and offers of support. A friend from church showed up early on the first morning to tell me he was headed to the site to look for Bruce.

Day after day people stopped by.

Many times, I greeted them at my fence to ward off any problems with my dog and to keep those conversations out of earshot of my daughters. Typically when someone stopped by Buster would position himself between me and the person. If the girls were outside, he would switch to standing between them and the visitor. He rarely barked at visitors. Just staring at you was enough to get his point across—don't mess with my girls.

A rumor spread that "Ann isn't doing well! She won't let anyone in her house!" Actually, if you were coming for a visit, of course you were invited in, but if you were just dropping off something for the aforementioned reasons, you probably didn't get in. That was strictly to protect you from my dog and guard my kids' privacy.

By Sunday my house was full of people with the best of intentions, but it became too much. My friend and pastor, Steve Shomo, stepped in and suggested daily guidelines to Christine.

"Ann doesn't answer the door or phone."

"Ann takes a nap every day."

"Ann eats three meals a day."

The time for circling the wagons had come.

My baby sister emerged as my protector. If you wanted to talk to me, you would have to get past her unless you were on the list. Yes, there was a pen–and–paper list of people.

Originally the list consisted of people who needed to be contacted and/or people who I needed to hear from for encouragement. On Sunday, it changed to a list of who had access to me.

Within days the list grew into a spiral notebook full of tasks to complete, contact information for the FDNY and NYPD as well as a quick resource of phone numbers for friends and family.

I started printing emails and placing them in a three-ring binder so Bruce could see them when he came home. The emails from friends, family, and associates brought comfort. Printing those emails gave me confidence that Bruce would see them.

One of those emails was from a young man who had spent the night in our pop–up trailer. Some people bring home stray cats or dogs, but Bruce brought home hikers. Hikers who were hiking the entire Appalachian Trail (A.T.) from Georgia to Maine were called thru hikers. The A.T. runs through Greenwood Lake so in the summer months there were hikers invited to sleep in our yard or take a shower or both.

Bruce enjoyed hiking, and he wanted me to enjoy it too, but it wasn't my thing. I did play a role in his hiking ventures. I was the drop–off or pick–up person. On occasion the pick-up involved an extra passenger who became a guest for the evening.

On Father's Day 2001, Bruce had invited two young men to spend the night in our pop–up trailer and enjoy a hot shower and a home cooked meal. We were in the process of selling the pop–up, so it was already set up in our driveway.

In our conversation over dinner, we learned that one young man, David, was a doctoral candidate trying to finish the A.T. before beginning his studies, and the other was his cousin who had agreed to accompany him for a portion of the journey.

The dinner conversation also revealed that we were reading the same book—*The Prayer of Jabez* by Bruce Wilkerson, a tiny little book that had caused a big stir in Christian circles. Interesting discussion followed.

Bruce prayed for safe journey as they continued their hike.

David prayed a beautiful prayer for our family.

After dinner that evening, television news reports revealed a horrific fire in NYC in which three firefighters died in the line of duty.

The following Tuesday Bruce attended the funeral of one of those firefighters. That same day was Meghan's eighth–grade graduation. Bruce was running late and called home to see if Meghan was okay with him wearing his uniform to her graduation. She was.

Little did we know how precious the photos of Bruce in his uniform and Meghan in her cap and gown would become. The receipt of a simple email brought all those memories to mind.

Professor Fischer was another person who sent an email. Back in the mid 70s, Bruce had taken some business and arboriculture classes at Bergen Community College. School was never Bruce's thing. Professor Fisher had mentored Bruce at a time when Bruce was starting his own arboriculture business. Sometimes when a customer wanted a tree taken down that didn't need to come down, Bruce talked himself out of work because he valued trees. The professor had proved to be a great encourager.

Even as a firefighter, Bruce had his second job as an arborist. Many firefighters have second jobs. Their schedules leave time to earn additional funds and their salaries leave a need for those extra funds.

Some of Bruce's tree customers knew his main job was a New York City firefighter but others didn't which made for some uncomfortable conversations as to why Bruce wasn't available to return calls for tree work after September 11, 2001.

* * *

There wasn't a specific moment when I knew Bruce was dead. As the days dragged on, I knew I had to make choices to be prepared if the worst happened.

I had a dream sometime during the first week. I dreamt Bruce was in one of the towers. Pretty high up and they came across injured civilians.

Suddenly there was the sound of floors collapsing one on top of another. Pancaking—boom, boom.

Bruce starting yelling "go, go, get out of here."

He turned to his fellow firefighters "Do you know God?"

He whispered, "I love you, girls." Girls is what Bruce called Emily, Meghan, and me. And then he was gone.

In the dream I had this sense he was face to face with God. Unafraid. He was okay. I wasn't afraid after the dream even though I had no idea what the dream meant.

Later in conversations with firefighters someone mentioned that the firefighters heard the floors collapsing before the building collapsed. I didn't mention the dream but took that as confirmation maybe it was more than a dream.

Maybe it was a revelation from God.

THE PILE

After an attack of any kind smashes the foundations of your life, before you can regain your bearings, you may find yourself staring at a massive pile of rubble.

In the aftermath of any tragedy, everything is upended. Routines, traditions, habits, memories, schedules. Plus, there is a pile of stuff that needs to be dealt with: paperwork, treatments, funerals, keepsakes.

Stuff that has to get done.

It can be both a curse and blessing, adding to the pain but distracting from the pain at the same time.

- The media called the destroyed World Trade Center site Ground Zero. Rescue workers called it the Pile.
- Imagine two 110–story buildings collapsing to form a pile approximately twelve stories tall.
- The rescue effort began immediately.
- No one was pulled out alive after Wednesday, September 12.
- A week later the heavy equipment was brought in.
- The site went from rescue to recovery.

4

MANHATTAN AND MEETINGS

There were practical issues that needed to be addressed. Bruce's car was fifty miles away at the firehouse in the Bronx. Parking is always at a premium in the city, and I understood having Bruce's car just hanging out in the Bronx wasn't helpful to Squad 41.

I also knew they weren't going to ask me to move it, so I asked Pastor Steve to arrange to get Bruce's car back to Greenwood Lake. I knew this was a big ask as it would be at least a half-day errand and involve more than just Pastor Steve. Pastor Steve recruited the perfect person to accompany him—Rod, a church member, and New York police officer stationed in the Bronx.

Pastor Steve and Rod not only brought the car home but also some personal items belonging to Bruce. Pastor Steve and

I were having coffee at my kitchen table when he gave me the items.

Until then, I hadn't given much thought to the whereabouts of Bruce's wallet, wedding ring, or watch but as Pastor Steve laid them on table before me, I remembered Bruce telling me that firefighters often leave their personal items in their locker when responding to a fire.

"I wasn't really sure what to expect when we went to the firehouse to get the car," Pastor Steve shared. "We knocked on the firehouse door, explained who we were, and they invited us in. They offered Rod and I coffee. Shared a few stories about Bruce. They seemed like they really needed to talk."

"Coffee and food are a big deal in the firehouse," I added.

"Then a couple of the guys went to get the stuff out of Bruce's locker. They took such care when they handed me his wallet and ring. Let me show you." Pastor Steve picked up the items from the table and stood. Tenderly with both hands he held the wallet, with the watch and ring balanced on top. "It was almost like presenting the rings in a wedding ceremony. Beautiful."

I was struck by the respect that was shown to these everyday items that belonged to my husband.

I eventually had my and Bruce's wedding rings sized to fit Emily and Meghan. I wore the anniversary ring Bruce had given me on my left ring finger. I felt that our marriage ended with his death, but our love continued.

In the course of time, I stopped wearing even the anniversary ring. Unfortunately, the ring didn't fit on my right hand, and wearing it on my left hand led to questions that had awkward answers.

Charlie stopped by and informed me of an FDNY meeting in Manhattan on Tuesday, September 18. He wasn't available to escort me but offered to find me an escort.

Manhattan had been my stomping grounds during my teens and twenties. In recent years, I'd taken trips into the city for Christmas–decoration viewing or museum trips with my girls. I knew I could get myself into the city. I didn't see the need for an FDNY escort.

Later that same day, sitting in the living room with my sister and daughters, I told them about the meeting.

"The FDNY is holding a meeting with the mayor and governor, and we've been invited to go."

"What's the meeting for?" Emily asked.

"I don't have the details yet, sweetheart.

Emily said, "Mom, if it has to do with Daddy, I want to come."

"I've already talked to Auntie Carol, and she said you guys could stay at her house. Uncle Tony is going to drive me and Aunt Christine in. But if you want to come, Emily, of course you can."

"Can I just stay at Auntie Carol's?" asked Meghan.

"Definitely."

We had a plan.

We knew the time of the meeting but not the exact location. It was all quite mysterious. We were supposed to report to one of the various gathering spots from where we would be moved to the actual meeting.

I supposed the intention was two-fold—first, to keep the media away and then to protect the identity and privacy of the family members.

As much as I didn't feel I needed an FDNY escort, I did feel the need to represent my firefighter husband in an honoring way. I carefully choose my attire to show respect for the importance of a meeting that would be attended by the governor, mayor, and other city officials. I chose dress pants and a jacket. Emily wore dress pants and a nice blouse.

* * *

The drive into the city was surreal. Men in full military garb with the biggest guns I had ever seen guarded the George Washington Bridge. I felt like I had been transported to another country. *We don't have military on our bridges. This is the United States of America.*

Looking at the empty skyline, I had no idea where the towers had stood just last week. They had been south of the Empire State Building, but where?

Apparently, Christine was thinking the same thing. She said, "I thought I would know where they had been. Like there would be a cardboard cut-out or something."

We chose the Fire Zone at Rockefeller Center as our meeting spot. We were met by concerned helpers who offered us cups of water, cookies, restrooms, and assurances that the buses would arrive shortly.

Plainclothes police officers directed us to the buses as they received instructions in their earpieces and spoke into their sleeves.

"Mom, it feels like we're in a bad spy movie," Emily whispered as we crossed the closed off street.

Boarding the bus, I saw faces sporting a dazed look that undoubtedly mirrored my own. Most people had family or friends with them, and my heart was deeply saddened at the sight of a young man who was all alone. *Is he representing his dad? He is too young to have to be the man of the family.*

The bus drove a few blocks to a large hotel.

As we rode the escalator up to the mezzanine level, Emily and I made eye contact. I gave her a weak smile. *How I wish my daughter wasn't experiencing this but oh, how proud I am of her.*

We entered a ballroom stripped bare except for round tables with white tablecloths and chairs. Claiming four empty seats, we introduced ourselves to our tablemates. They were the fiancée of a firefighter and the wife and grown children of an FDNY officer.

Mayor Giuliani, Governor Pataki, Commissioner Thomas Von Essen from the FDNY, and the medical examiner spoke. The purpose of the meeting was to inform us that the mission was changing from rescue to recovery. They had found no one alive in days so it was time to change the focus. Heavy equipment would be brought in to move the debris.

I had known these words were coming. My emotions were still on autopilot, but the words were still stunning. I thought about looking at Emily but couldn't—I was just trying to hold myself together.

There was discussion about DNA samples and opportunity to give DNA before you left.

In the years since this meeting, some FDNY widows have come to call it "the leave–your–DNA–at–the–door meeting."

The formal meeting was followed by time for questions and answers, during which many people, myself included, wandered around searching for familiar faces.

I eventually spied the other wives from Squad 41. I cautiously approached them. Even though our husbands had worked together, I didn't really know these women as personal friends. We were all navigating this terrible event, but not together. I walked up to one of the women.

"Hi, I'm Ann Van Hine, Bruce's wife."

"Oh, Ann. Good to see you."

Hugs were exchanged.

"This is my sister, Christine," I said as Christine and Emily joined me. "And my daughter, Emily."

More hugs.

Polite conversation.

A promise to pray for each other.

Then suddenly I said, "Why don't we pray right now?"

Did I just say that out loud?

They nodded.

"I'll be right back," I said. "Get your families."

As the other women rounded up their loved ones, I hurried back to our table and found Tony.

"Tony, you have to come with me. I told the other women from Squad 41 you would pray for them."

Even today, years later, the memory of that moment is so vivid in my mind. I'm standing in this large ballroom, the noise level is high, there are people all around, the commissioner of the FDNY is onstage answering questions, and we (Squad 41 and families) are holding hands in a circle.

And for a moment the other voices in the room fade away, and there is only this circle of people and Tony's voice offering a prayer of hope.

Amen.

After Tony's prayer, there were more hugs and promises to stay in touch.

We stayed a little longer and then headed to the parking garage.

On the ride home we discussed the DNA testing that we needed to accomplish.

I didn't say it out loud, but I knew the next step I had to take.

Bruce wasn't coming home. We didn't have his body. We would probably never have his body.

I needed to pronounce him dead.

As the wife of a firefighter, I had lived with the possibility that Bruce could be killed in the line of duty. It wasn't something I constantly thought about, but it had always been in the back of my mind. Just below the surface.

Crying in the shower when I heard of a firefighter's death anywhere in the country was one of my ways of dealing and being so grateful that it wasn't my husband.

But now it was my husband who had died.

The current circumstances were not something I had ever imagined. Not something I could ever have dreamed. Standing by a bed in the burn unit and saying *I love you* was how I thought it might play out. But having to fill out a missing person report and pronouncing him dead? Not in my wildest dreams.

Sometimes we talked about our wishes should one of us die. I remembered one such conversation as we drove home from a funeral.

I had asked, "When a Christian dies, shouldn't the funeral look and feel different than that of a nonbeliever?"

"Yeah, it should," Bruce had replied.

"I don't mean it won't be sad, but if we truly believe what we *say* we believe, then it should be different."

"You would think."

"On a different note," I had added, "I don't want the mayor at your funeral."

"What?"

"The mayor doesn't even know you!"

"What are we talking about?" he'd laughed.

"Line of duty funerals. If you die in the line of duty, I don't want the mayor there."

"That will be your problem." He had flashed me a big grin. "Because I won't be there. I'll be dead."

I'd smiled and motioned like I was hitting him up the side of the head.

Now that my worst fear had come true, I was experiencing the power and strength of the "brotherhood." I still didn't understand it. But I wanted to respect it. I wanted to do what Bruce as a firefighter would have wanted, but I also wanted to do what was right for our family.

When Christine got back from taking the girls to school the morning after the Manhattan meeting, I told her it was time to have a memorial service.

She agreed.

I decided I needed the acceptance and blessing of three groups of people before I made any hard plans: my daughters, my mother-in-law, and the Squad 41 firefighters.

In a phone conversation with my sister-in-law, I learned that Bruce's mom had scheduled a meeting with her lawyer to change her will. I took that as a sign that she assumed Bruce was dead.

I mentioned to Charlie that I wanted to have a memorial service. He assured me that it was up to me, but that the fire department hadn't given up hope of finding the guys.

That evening, Christine and I sat on the living room floor with Emily and Meghan. "Where do you think Daddy is right now?" I asked.

"Heaven," both girls responded at the same time.

"Then it is time we plan a memorial service."

"But what if we are wrong?" Emily asked. "What if they find Daddy?"

"I would like nothing better than for Daddy to walk into his own service. Whatever happens, it still feels like it's time."

By Friday, September 20, as most Americans were starting to resume their normal lives, we were slowly putting one foot in front of the other. We were still living with the immediate focus of what needed to be accomplished day by day.

Most days Emily and Meghan attended school. Our church set up a schedule for meals and an information source on the church website. Carol postponed the start of new classes at the studio. I postponed my other teaching commitments to the first week of October. In the meantime, Christine and I tried to figure out what needed to be done for the service and life in general.

Someone from Squad 41 called twice a day. Firefighters were still arriving on my doorstep.

One afternoon Captain Vomero from Squad 41 and a few of the firefighters came to the house. We sat around the kitchen table and drank coffee as they offered assurances that they were doing their best to find "the guys."

One evening two firefighters, both named Jim, came and shared stories of Bruce's adventures and antics at Engine 79/Truck 37, Bruce's first firehouse.

"So, we're on this job," said Jim #1, grinning at Emily and Meghan, "and your dad is the irons man. That's the guy who carries the Halligan tool and the other tools for prying doors open. As we are packing up, the tools are on your Dad's shoulder and he swings around." He paused for effect. "And BOOM! The tools hit the battalion chief right in the mouth. Blood everywhere."

Emily and Meghan gasped.

Jim #2 continued the story. "The chief is rushed to hospital. Your dad is pretty sure his career is over!"

Jim #1 chimed back in. "At the hospital, doctors find that the chief has cancer. Never would have known if your Dad hadn't knocked his teeth out. The chief actually credits your dad with saving his life."

The stories continued, filling the room with laughter for hours.

Such a welcome sound.

* * *

As I continued with my plans for the memorial service, my pastor, family, and friends shared thoughts and opinions. But the main voices I listened to were my own, Emily's, and Meghan's.

We decided to hold the service on Saturday, September 29. And we chose *not* to hold it at our home church as I didn't want the girls reminded of their daddy's memorial service every Sunday.

I chose Maranatha Church of the Nazarene in Paramus, New Jersey, as the funeral location. Maranatha was bigger, more centrally located than our church, and had been our home church for many years. Bruce and I were married there when it was in New Milford before it moved to a bigger location. And Emily had been the first baby dedicated in the new building.

We decided to prepare a printed worship booklet. Mom Van Hine went right to work finding Bruce's childhood photos. My mom supplied the photo taken of Meghan and Bruce at her eighth–grade graduation.

We all sorted through albums and boxes to find photos that would tell Bruce's life story not only as a firefighter but as a hiker, tree guy, and most importantly as a son, brother, husband, father, and friend.

As we sat around the kitchen table looking at photos, we also chose songs and readings. Then we discussed who should speak.

"Pastor Steve will speak. Who else?" I asked.

"Uncle Craig or Charlie," suggested Emily.

"I'll ask them. Anyone else?"

"Pastor Jerry," added Meghan. "He was a firefighter before he was a pastor. He knew Daddy. Do you think we should ask Grandma's pastor to read something? She would like that."

"That's a nice idea, Meghan." I nodded. "I will mention it to Grandma. You know what? I think we need a secret code word in case things get weird." I didn't even know what I meant but felt it was a good idea to have a phrase if Emily or Meghan needed my immediate attention during the service or reception.

We kicked around a few ideas and landed on "bubble moment." In a comic strip, a bubble over someone's head reveals what they are *really* thinking (whether or not they say the words out loud!). If the girls said the code word, I'd know they had something they needed to share with me immediately and privately.

Slowly the service was coming together.

Instead of having people sign a guest book, we decided to include a postcard in the worship folder. The postcard had our address on one side and a place to share a memory or thought on the other.

Sometimes planning all the little details of the service felt overwhelming—but they were a welcome distraction, too.

I need to get a basket for the postcards. Maybe two baskets? What am I going to wear? What are the girls going to wear? Should we have a bagpiper? What about a reception afterwards? Cheesecake and coffee? Do I really have to do this?

5

THE SITE AND THE SERVICE

The FDNY had given families of first responders permission to visit Ground Zero, which was not, of course, accessible to the general public. I knew some people who had headed to the site within hours of the attacks.

I didn't feel the need to go. I felt the FDNY was taking care of finding Bruce. I needed to take care of my girls. At the same time, I didn't want to regret *not* going. Some things have no do-overs. At some point there'd be no more opportunity to visit the site and see the destruction, so the girls and I decided to go the day before Bruce's memorial service.

The Family Assistance Unit of the FDNY had left a fifteen–seat passenger van at my house in case we needed it. (One firefighter had jokingly said, "Take your girls to the mall in it." *I don't think so).*

On Friday, September 28, we piled into that van to make the journey to the Brooklyn Navy Yard. The military still guarded the bridges. The traffic moved at a snail's pace. When we finally arrived in Brooklyn, a huge dump truck blocked the entrance to a street that was no longer accessible. I could still smell smoke.

The military presence, smoke, and blocked streets had transformed a familiar setting into something you might see in an old news reel. I felt like I was in a foreign country.

At the Brooklyn Navy Yard after identifications had been checked, we were escorted to a party boat that looked sad. The boat was in fine shape but there were no flickering lights or people in party attire—just us and another family that looked shell-shocked. We were joined by FDNY, NYPD, and Red Cross personnel.

We were given a brown–bag lunch that had been packed by school children and included crayon drawings. The NYPD chaplain visited each family and offered words of condolences and support.

The Red Cross volunteer gave Emily and Meghan teddy bears and handed out little packets of tissues.

"Look," I said, "the Red Cross has tissues with their logo. I guess they hand these out at all kinds of disasters." Then I winced. *Okay, that wasn't a normal comment. Get it together. You can do this. You have to do this. Greater is He who is in you than He that is in the world.*

When we arrived at the marina in Manhattan, we saw sheets of white paper scattered everywhere and a row of small sailboats covered in gray ash. The other family on our boat included a pregnant woman. Before disembarking she was given a paper mask.

A plywood walkway led to the site. We followed our escorts as Meghan walked with Christine, and I walked with Emily. My sister Barbara had flown in from California, and she walked with Christine's husband Arend.

I remember thinking, *Everyone is taken care of.*

Ash covered everything and seemed to hang in the air. The experience felt bizarre, not knowing where I was or even why I was here, not to mention being escorted by uniformed police officers and firefighters.

As we walked past, I noticed that people wearing hats removed them. They stopped talking. They nodded.

They know. We are the families of the lost.

After we arrived at the viewing corner on Liberty and West Streets, our escorts distributed a map of the World Trade Center marked with an arrow and the words "You are here."

But no map could help me grasp what I was seeing: heavy equipment—dump trucks, all forms of construction equipment—digging, lifting, and moving twisted pieces of steel.

The smoke hung in the air as it rose from the pile.

The noise reverberated all around me—and inside my head, too.

Suddenly Meghan burst into tears. I held my fourteen–year–old daughter, cried with her, and whispered in her ear words of love. I squeezed her tightly and tried to protect her from the reality all around us, but I couldn't.

The NYPD chaplain began reading Psalm 23:

The Lord is my Shepherd, I shall not want. He makes me lie down in green pastures, he leads me beside still waters, he restores my soul. He guides me along the paths of righteousness for his name's sake. Even though I walk through the valley of the shadow of death, I will fear no evil, for you are with me; your rod and your staff, they comfort me. You prepare a table before me in the presence of my enemies. You anoint my head with oil, my cup overflows. Surely your goodness and love will follow me all the days of my life, and I will dwell in the house of the Lord forever.

Then he said, "I am going to recite the Lord's Prayer. You are welcome to join me."

I joined in. "Our Father which art in heaven hallowed be your name. Your kingdom come, your will be done on earth as it is in heaven. Give us this day our daily bread and forgive us our trespasses as we forgive those who trespass against us. Leading us not into temptation but deliver us from evil. . . "

Scripture had just been spoken in the middle of the World Financial Center and no one said, "Are we allowed to do that?"

I remembered God's promise in scripture: "My word will not return void."

Thank you, Lord.

We were hoping to visit Bruce's firehouse in the Bronx. On a good day, getting to the Bronx from Manhattan is an adventure. Considering we had to go back to Brooklyn via boat before we could even begin the trek to the Bronx, we were in for a long journey.

I turned to Aldo, our Squad 41 escort. "Is it possible for us to stop by Squad 41?"

"No problem," he assured me. "We will make it happen." And he did.

When we arrived at Squad 41, two official–looking men in suits were exiting their black town car.

"Wait here. I will be right back," said Aldo as he jumped out of the van.

He spoke for a moment to the two men before returning to my side of the van. I unrolled my window.

"They're city officials who are here to learn a little bit about Bruce before attending his service tomorrow. Is that okay with you?"

"Of course," I said, looking over his shoulder at the two men. The shock of running into the widow and her children was visible on their faces. I felt bad. I realized that, under the circumstances, my presence could suck the air out of a room.

The next morning, Saturday, September 29, I heard a knock on the kitchen door. I peeked out the curtain and saw Pastor Steve smiling back at me.

"Come in." I opened the door and waved him inside. "Would you like some coffee?"

"No thanks. I just wanted to tell you that I'm going for it." He went on to explain that he planned on presenting the gospel message in the sermon he would be delivering at Bruce's service in a couple of hours. He wanted to talk about not only Bruce's faith, but that Jesus is the way to salvation for anyone. "I wanted you to know. Are you okay with that?"

"Absolutely. It's what Bruce would've wanted. It's what I want." As I spoke, I realized this was our *if we truly believe what we say we believe it better be different* opportunity.

"Good. Well, I'm going to head down to Maranatha. See you later."

"See you later. Thank you."

A few hours later John Gallagher, a firefighter from West Point, escorted my girls, Christine, her husband, and I into the fifteen–passenger van. We picked up my parents and headed to the church.

When we arrived at Maranatha a huge American flag hung between two fire department ladder trucks. Firefighters had started to gather. We waited in Pastor Charlie's office with those who would be speaking.

When I realized I had left my Bible in the van, Pastor Charlie handed me his Bible. I was struck by a sense of profound gratitude and comfort. It seemed appropriate, since he was the man for many years who had given me the Bible every week in his Sunday sermons.

While Jon Werking played the prelude, we entered the sanctuary. I wanted to gaze around and see who was there, but that felt a little like peeking out from behind the curtain before a dance performance. I'd always told my students that was a big no-no.

The firefighters who had been waiting outside filed in to take their seats. Almost immediately someone started clapping. Eventually Jon stopped playing as everyone stood and applauded the firefighters. The stress of the last weeks was evident on their faces, and my heart broke for them.

The honor guard entered carrying various flags.

Pastor Steve and the worship team from my home church led the congregation in singing "The Church's One Foundation."

I love this hymn, I thought as a special memory from June 2001 filled my mind. Along with 20,000 other believers, we were attending the Sunday morning worship service at General Assembly for the Church of the Nazarene. During worship, the words for all the hymns and choruses had been projected on the screens. Except for one song.

The last song: "The Church's One Foundation."

The assumption was everyone knew the words to that hymn. It is considered a standard in the church.

But my girls didn't know the words. In fact, they had never heard the song before.

Bruce and I were shocked.

"What do you mean you never heard that song before?" I asked them.

After we repeated that story to Pastor Steve, the old hymns began to appear in the Sunday song list.

On the day of Bruce's memorial service, that special hymn set the tone for the rest of the afternoon.

After worship, Pastor Steve welcomed everyone, saying, "We are here today to remember Richard Bruce Van Hine, who was a husband, father, brother, son, faithful friend, member of the greatest fire department in the world, committed church member, and most importantly a follower of the Lord Jesus Christ."

The clergy who spoke were all those who had spoken truth into our lives through the years. These were men and women who knew Bruce.

Pastor Jerry had been a member of the FDNY for thirty years. He and Bruce hadn't been on the department at the same time, but that brotherhood bond was real.

He was visibly shaken as he shared from the pulpit, "I am hurting today."

Pastor Maureen Garcia, my mentor and friend, shared a George McDonald quote: "Instead of asking yourself whether you believe or not, ask yourself whether you have this day done one thing because He said, 'Do it,' or once abstained because He said, 'Do not do it.' It is simply absurd to say you believe, or even want to believe in Him, if you do not do anything He tells you."

Dr. Dale Noel, a gentle and unassuming church friend and hiking buddy of Bruce's, offered a beautiful prayer. As part of his prayer, he quoted 2 Timothy 4:7: "I have fought the good fight, I have finished the race, I have kept the faith."

Pastor Steve would later mention that same verse and personalize it by saying, "Bruce fought the fight, Bruce finished the race, Bruce kept the faith."

Charlie and Craig offered words of tribute.

Charlie mentioned he had only known Bruce for five years but felt like he had always known him. It seemed as if they had lived parallel lives, both starting tree businesses in the 1970s before becoming firefighters. Charlie spoke of tree work, hiking, firefighting, and faith. He got a laugh from stating, "In the fire department we say to be abused is to be loved. Bruce was definitely loved."

Charlie closed with 1 Thessalonians 4: "Make it your ambition to lead a quiet life: You should mind your own business and work with your hands, just as we told you, so that your daily life may win the respect of outsiders and so that you will not be dependent on anybody."

I smiled when I heard him quote those verses as he didn't know they were a favorite of mine. As a kindergarten aide, I had often told little tattletales, "Did you know 'mind your own business' is in the Bible?"

Craig, on the other hand, had known Bruce all of his life. Bruce's parents and Craig's parents had been friends since the 1930s, long before Craig and Bruce were twinkles in their daddies' eyes. Craig and Bruce grew up together. In fact, Craig introduced me to Bruce. Craig spoke of Bruce as a loyal friend and a keeper of secrets. If you told Bruce something in confidence, he didn't repeat it.

Then it was my turn to speak. I walked to the platform trying not to make eye contact with anyone.

There was a coin imprinted in the podium and rubbing my finger over it felt real, felt solid.

"To the firefighters, thank you for how you have cared for us. To the firefighters' wives and girlfriends, we need to sit and have tea soon. To my friends and family, I want to say I have no regrets. To my church family, thank you and I think I have gained a few pounds."

There were a few chuckles.

"Different thoughts have come to mind about what I want to say to you, but I haven't written anything down. Here goes. This past June, we went on a family trip to Indianapolis for

General Assembly for the Church of the Nazarene. I'd gone to General Assembly four years earlier. It was such a wonderful time with God, I felt Him stir in my heart a desire to bring Bruce and our girls back with me if I ever had the chance to go again. So when I had the opportunity to return, we decided to make it a family adventure. Because Meghan's eighth–grade graduation was Tuesday and I needed to be in Indianapolis on Wednesday, we made it a *real* adventure and drove overnight. I can tell you two things I learned from driving overnight: it's very dark and there are lots of big trucks. When we arrived, I gave the girls and Bruce the schedules I'd made for them because, well, I'm a planner."

I spotted a few dear friends who knew me best nodding their heads.

"Within hours," I continued, "the girls and Bruce had made different plans. I was disappointed, and as I prayed, the still small voice of God said, 'I told you to get them here. I didn't tell you to plan their days.' So, they did their own things, but dinners and evening service were together—and we had the best time."

I took a deep breath. "I believe the same is true today. Bruce got you here. Personally, I would have preferred a different way to get you here, but we showed you God. Now, what you do with that is your business. God is a gentleman. He will never force his way in. We showed you love. The Bible says God is love. So, you have seen God."

I returned to my seat during a standing ovation.

Pastor Steve gave a sermon entitled "Prepared In and Out of Season" in which he gave a strong Gospel message.

We sang one more song before the benediction.

At that point, Pastor Steve invited the two city officials to read letters from the mayor and the governor. I got my wish that the mayor wasn't present. Not because I told him not to come, but because there were so many funerals for him to attend.

Before the colors were retired, Captain Vomero of Squad 41 presented Emily with a memorial firefighter helmet, as Charlie handed Bruce's dress hat to Meghan.

Years ago, Meghan had added a piece of paper to the inside of Bruce's hat so that when he took it off, he would see it. It said, "I love you, Dad" and was signed "Megs." That note was still there.

Captain Vomero instructed the firefighters to file out. Again, there was a standing ovation and thunderous applause. And then Emily, Meghan, and I walked out the side door followed by my family. I felt like I was leading a parade.

Outside the church, we were met by a silence that was almost palpable. As I walked around to the front of the church toward the firefighters standing in formation, I heard only one sound: my heels on the pavement.

The firefighters stared straight ahead as I passed them wearing a weak smile. There were people standing across the street, but what I remember most of all was that silence.

Silence except for the click, click of my shoes on the pavement.

There was no bagpiper. I had decided the sound of bagpipe music was something I couldn't prepare myself to hear.

That would've been too much.

The girls, my parents, and I reentered the church through a downstairs walkway en route to the reception. There, friends and family were already helping themselves to cheesecake from the Bronx and coffee—Bruce's favorites.

After the reception we headed with a small group of family and friends to Carol's house for dinner.

We had survived.

No bubble moments.

The reality that our personal loss was part of something so much bigger was reinforced by excerpts of Bruce's memorial service being aired on the evening news and mentioned in the newspaper.

The attendance postcards gave us a true sense of who was present. Firefighters from all over the region had attended. Many postcards were placed in the baskets. Many more arrived in the mail for weeks.

The fact that people took the time to share stories and encouragement wasn't lost on us.

6

A NEW NORMAL, TAKE 1

∞

On Monday October 1, 2001, we took the first tiny steps to gather up familiar pieces of our lives prior to September 11. Everything had changed, even though so much was the same.

We called it our *new normal*, which is what we got as we started putting one foot in front of the other. We had to embrace a new pattern for our lives—not better or even worse— just different.

Christine headed back to Schenectady, the girls went off to school, and the New School of Dance Arts opened for its twenty-sixth season.

Teaching dance wasn't a nine–to–five job. I would teach a morning class or two, teach an early afternoon class, and then teach three or four classes after school. Most days I was at the studio early because the girls needed to be at school at 8:00 a.m.

This allowed me to take care of the business end of things or work on choreography.

Typically, my first class started at 9:30 or 10 a.m. and my last class finished at 7 or 7:30 p.m. followed by a forty-five–minute commute home.

My schedule allowed for errands between classes, visits to see my folks, or talks and tea with my best friend Carol when she was at the studio at the same time.

Teaching dance was a wonderful vocation. The days could be long, but the bonus was that I had my summers and school holidays off.

My classes on Monday October 1 included new students as well as girls I had known for years. A wonderful perk of teaching dance is that you have the privilege of being a part of a child's life for years. Many of the girls had started dancing at four years old—and now some of them were seniors in high school. So to say I knew these girls and they knew me would be an understatement.

I invited everyone to sit on the floor and asked them the same questions I asked every first class of the season: "How was your summer? Did you do anything special?"

After they had filled me in on their summers, I filled them in on mine.

"I had a great summer," I said, "but my September wasn't so good." I smiled weakly. "But what has happened doesn't change who I am to you, or who you are to me."

I paused and intentionally looked each of them in the eye. "I am okay. We are going to be okay." And then I added, "So, everybody up! Let's get busy."

Emily and Meghan were students in those classes. They chose not to attend that first day, and I was grateful. As *Miss Ann,* I could articulate those thoughts but to express them as *Mom* would have been too hard.

As I'd often told Emily and Meghan, lots of kids might call me *Miss Ann,* but only two kids in the whole world call me *Mom.*

The first day went well. But on the second day of being back at work, as I pulled into the driveway, I realized I had forgotten to ask anyone to let the dog out.

"Oh, no, this is never going to work," I moaned. "I can't do this. I can't even make sure the dog is let out."

As I let myself into the house, I sniffed and peered. Surprisingly, there was no puddle of pee on the kitchen floor. *Good dog!* I thought to myself.

Just then the phone rang.

It was my neighbor. "Ann, I just wanted you to know I let Buster out. Hope that was okay. You didn't ask, but I saw you weren't home."

Great neighbor.

In the coming weeks, sometimes on trash day when I arrived home my garbage cans had already been lugged from the street back up to my garage. The girls and I joked that there was a garbage-can fairy in the neighborhood. Years later, the same neighbor who so many times took care of letting Buster out admitted she took care of my garbage cans as well.

Remarkable neighbor.

Despite the compassion of people who cared for me during that painful season, there were many times I felt like I'd been cast in an episode of a police drama like *CSI*.

I hadn't even auditioned for the part, but here I was. Furthermore, I felt like the whole world was watching and expecting a brilliant performance.

But I didn't know my lines. In fact, I hadn't seen the script.

This performance was way beyond my realm of knowledge and experience. And all those acting and dancing lessons from my youth weren't going to help.

This was real life—though it didn't feel like my life at all.

Besides my new role, I had a new name: Mrs. Van Hine.

When Bruce and I married, I had already owned my studio for five years and was well-known in the community. I decided to keep my maiden name and added Van Hine, so my legal name became Ann Collette Clark-Van Hine.

At my studio, I was known as Ann Clark or Miss Ann. Even at church I was Miss Ann. No one referred to me by my married last name. In fact, Bruce was more likely to be called Mr. Clark than I was to be called Mrs. Van Hine.

But now I was Mrs. Van Hine, FDNY widow.

* * *

As my FDNY family liaison, there were few things that Charlie insisted I do. But visiting the Family Assistance Center at Pier 94 was one of them. In fact, he was very persistent.

But I kept putting him off.

I didn't feel like I needed assistance. I had a tremendous support system, and I didn't want help that might be given to other people who had less support than I did.

I have my work.

I am not a victim.

My girls are not victims.

Bruce is not a victim. He died in the line of duty. He gave his life; no one took it.

I know why my husband died on September 11, 2001. He was a New York City Firefighter doing his job.

Charlie kept bringing it up, which confused me. What did I need to do at Pier 94 that I hadn't already done?

Christine and I had already completed the missing person's report one morning while the girls were at school.

Emily and I had already visited a local lab to have our cheeks swabbed for DNA.

Christine and I had even visited a lawyer friend of hers to do paperwork for the death certificate.

I couldn't imagine what else needed to be done.

But Charlie didn't give up.

At the end of October, Christine, Emily, and I planned a trip to Pier 94.

I would go.

But on my terms.

I didn't want to go in a fire department vehicle or have a fire department escort because I knew that would get me special treatment.

We drove ourselves into Manhattan, parked near Pier 94, and walked over, joining the end of a line outside the building.

Within moments, someone greeted us and asked: "Why are you here today?"

I explained. "The FDNY suggested I come. My husband was one of the firefighters lost during the attacks."

"Oh, follow me." And we were promptly escorted to the front of the line.

That was exactly the kind of special treatment I hadn't wanted.

"Thank you," I said anyway.

The Family Assistance Center was set up like a convention center. It was open to anyone who needed help. There were booths representing the FDNY, NYPD, New York State Crimes Victim Board/Safe Horizons, Veterans Administration, American Red Cross, and the Salvation Army. Even the Buddhists had a booth.

Visitors were offered meals, childcare, medical and mental health services, and access to various government agencies and non-government organizations as well.

We started at the FDNY booth. From there we were directed to the New York State Crimes Victim Board/Safe Horizons booth.

After mentioning Bruce had been in the Navy, we were guided to the Veterans Administration to complete more paperwork. Thankfully, Charlie had given me a heads up about what kind of paperwork was needed for this visit to the Pier, so I had brought along what I would need.

As I finished up, the VA representative handed me a small cardboard box that contained an American flag. I thanked him. He directed me to the Disabled Veterans Booth.

We found that booth.

"Hi, I was told to come to see you to complete some paperwork," I said.

"Please have a seat," the woman replied.

"Thank you."

"Did they just hand you that box?"

"Yes, at the Veterans Administration booth."

"Oh, my. They didn't fold that flag for you. I'm sorry. This should never happen. Let me get someone to fold it properly."

I tried to reassure her it wasn't necessary, but she got up and hurried away.

Christine, Emily, and I exchanged confused glances. Within moments she was back with two men.

"I got someone to fold it properly." She said as she reached for the box, took the flag out and gave it to the two men.

Christine, Emily, and I watched in awe as the flag was folded in thirds, then in triangles until just the stars were showing.

They handed it back to me.

"Thank you."

We were then directed to the Red Cross and Salvation Army booths. Most times we were completing forms or receiving information on services they could offer.

People kept mentioning that we should visit the Buddhist booth. I felt a little weird about that as I am a Christian. After some thought, we found our way there. A Buddhist gentleman in a long flowing robe sat in front of an open checkbook. He simply asked my name and wrote me a check for $1,000.

I was stunned and totally humbled.

* * *

During those first weeks after the attacks, Doug and Rene drove the forty-five minutes to Greenwood Lake on a regular basis to help the girls with their homework. Doug and Bruce had been in Naval Reserves together. The four of us had vacationed together before kids.

When kids—three for them and two for us—came along, family sleepovers at their home or ours became our new tradition. We had dinner together, played board games, and then sent the children off to bed so the grownups could chat. What memorable times! After Bruce's death, having these dear friends show up to oversee homework and visit with me was above and beyond.

Carol continued to be a lifesaver as well. She lived within blocks of the girls' high school, and Meghan and Emily had frequent sleepovers at her house.

My parents were instrumental in transporting my girls from school to the studio or to their house to hang out while I taught. My mom provided endless cups of tea and meals.

My dad supplied the piece of advice that proved golden: "Don't make any major changes in your life for the first year." I have thought back on his advice many times and have shared it with others.

Daily, my mailbox was full of cards and notes from family, friends, and total strangers. Some of those cards were addressed to the family of Richard B. Van Hine, Greenwood Lake, New York. Newspapers all over the country had published the names and hometowns of the firefighters who had died, and Bruce's full name and the city where we lived were on those lists. Often, that was the only address people had. Nevertheless, cards without a street address were delivered to our home on a daily basis.

Sometimes firefighters would call or stop by and say, "I worked with Richard" or "I worked with Richie." That told me they had done a tour with him or been at the same fire, but they weren't close friends. If they were, they would have called him Bruce.

Cards with crayon drawings, homemade bookmarks, offers of prayer, and words of encouragement arrived by mail all through the fall. A school in South Dakota sent a quilt the students had made along with photos documenting the process.

Charlie stopped by weekly with items for me that had been delivered to Squad 41.

Individuals and corporations reached out.

In the mail one day there was a big package from the Philip Morris Company.

Cigarettes? I wondered.

Actually, it was a large round plastic storage container that looked like an enormous container of Tang. Emily and Meghan had never heard of Tang, but it made me smile.

"It's what the astronauts drink," I explained.

Upon opening the container, we found numerous Kraft Food items. Who knew Philip Morris owned Kraft? The container was perfect for storing Buster's dog food. The mac and cheese and other treats were appreciated and came in handy.

Many weekends, Christine drove down from Schenectady to hang out with us or help sort through paperwork. One Saturday morning as we sat at my rectangular kitchen table finishing our coffee, I said, "Christine, while you're here, can you help us rearrange some furniture?"

"Sure."

"I want to swap the round table that's in the corner of the living room with this one. And I want to move my bed to a different spot in my bedroom."

"Where are we starting?" she asked.

"Let's tackle the table first. Girls, come and help."

It required some tools and brute force, but we got it done. Now we could arrange the chairs at the kitchen table so there wasn't an empty spot. And my bedroom looked different. *Little steps.*

* * *

Auto-pilot is the best word to describe how I navigated the days, weeks, and months. I went to work, cared for my girls, sent thank you notes, got things done, and even attended some amazing events, but it was all done in a fog. As a matter of fact, I think some people got two thank you notes. Other people got none. To simply come up with a system for who still needed a note took too much brain power.

Usually, I love being sucked into a good book, but I didn't have the attention span. I tried reading magazines, but that was no better. The only thing I could read was the Bible. Short passages brought comfort.

Even though I was functioning in what felt like a trance I was grateful. Grateful that I had an amazing support system in my family, friends, the FDNY, and most importantly, God.

Before long, we were no longer hiding behind Him as much as walking with Him ever so slowly through each day.

* * *

One day Emily and Meghan came to me individually and asked me the same three questions:

"Can we still go to Eastern Christian?"

"Are we still going to live in this house?"

"What will happen when we get married?"

I gave them both the same answers: "I will do my best to keep you in EC. Yes, we are going to keep living in this house. And right now, we don't have to worry about when you get married because that is a long way off. You aren't allowed to date, and you don't even have a boyfriend."

The answer to the question "Can we still go to EC?" was answered in a mighty way when Eastern Christian High School set up a fund for Emily's and Meghan's tuition. Enough money was collected to pay for Emily's senior year and all four years of Meghan's education. There was even money left over to set aside to help other families suffering loss.

The teachers set up a separate fund that paid for my daughters' yearbooks, field trips, and proms. I was beyond grateful.

* * *

Bruce had been vigilant about maintaining our cars, but now that he was gone a reliable vehicle was a must.

Before long, colleagues, friends, and family had started the ball rolling to buy me a new car. Squad 41 raised a considerable amount of money, while other people made contributions in honor of Bruce. Pastor Steve, my financial guy Steve, and Bill—a friend who worked for Chrysler—spearheaded the effort. Before long, I was calling them my "car team."

Of course, I thought my car was fine. Our cars had always been hand-me-downs, used cars that started with a lot of miles and quickly gained more miles due to long commutes for both Bruce and me.

When asked what kind of car I wanted, I simply said, "Anything but a minivan!"

My car team picked out two cars for me to test drive.

I had never test driven a car before in my life.

As the salesperson handed me the keys, he said, "Drive it around town and let me know what you think."

I had no idea what to do next.

How do I know if this is the right car?

I'd never had a choice before. It wasn't in my scope of experiences or expertise.

So, I called my friend JoEllen who lived nearby and asked her to come along. After we drove around for a few minutes, I asked JoEllen if there was something special I should check.

She suggested looking under the hood. When we got back to her house, I parked the car and as I popped the hood, I turned to her and asked, "What are we supposed to look for?"

She said, "I don't know."

We stood for a few moments looking at the engine. Silence. I shrugged my shoulders. "Let's look in the trunk. As least we'll know if it's big enough."

I closed the hood.

We walked to the back of the car, opened the truck, and stared into the trunk.

JoEllen announced, "Looks good to me."

We both laughed.

In the end, I simply trusted that Pastor Steve and the other men knew what they were doing. All I knew is that I thought this car was the cuter of the two, so I became the proud owner of my first new car, a 2002 Sebring.

THE PIT

Eventually, after days, months, or even years, the pile diminishes until it is altogether gone. But something has taken its place.

You peer into a dark and cavernous space. It is a pit, a void left by what was taken from you.

A hole that remains long after the pile is gone.

Now what?

How do you fill the hole so you can feel whole again?

What can possibly occupy that sacred space?

How do you move forward?

- As the Pile got lower, it became known as the Pit.
- The recovery continued twenty-four hours a day, seven days a week.
- The last column of steel was removed on May 30, 2002.
- Signage was placed around the Pit to add clarity as to where the buildings had stood.
- The names of the lost were displayed.
- Visitors peered through the chain link fences into a massive concrete hole and tried to comprehend what had happened.

7

A NEW NORMAL, TAKE 2

Early on in this journey I had told Emily and Meghan that we didn't have to be *brave*. Daddy was one of New York's bravest; we're not. I had also told my daughters they were not defined by September 11, 2001. The September 11 attacks were something that happened to our nation and to our family. It wasn't who they were. They weren't children of 9/11.

At the same time, much of our lives *had* been redefined by 9/11. It goes without saying that the tremendous loss of a husband and father had changed our lives forever. But our lives had been impacted in other ways, too—including our schedules and even our social life.

For example, there were constant invitations to sporting events, concerts, remembrance events, or all three in a single weekend. Being connected to the September 11 attacks had opened the door to endless opportunities—just as I was working hard to reestablish our basic everyday life.

I found myself trying to navigate when to say yes, when to say no, who we might offend if we declined, and simply when was it all too much:

Giants training camp at the Meadowlands might be fun for the girls to do with their youth group leader. There's also a Random House book event at Chelsea Piers with ice skating. Should we do that, too? The Random House event means driving into the city again. Am I ready to do that? Should we just stay home instead?

We appreciated the invitations. We enjoyed the experiences. And even though we couldn't say yes all the time, when we did accept an invitation, it was often a nice distraction.

But even then, the stark reality was Bruce was gone. And nothing could change that.

*   *   *

By mid-fall, we accepted an invitation to attend The Concert for New York City at Madison Square Garden (MSG). The benefit concert was attended by many first responders and families of the lost.

Since I had never been to a rock concert before, I asked my brother and sister-in-law to come along. Recently James and Fran had moved back to New Jersey from California where they had lived for several years. Their return to the East Coast couldn't have come at a better time.

My little brother James was a rock concert veteran. He was younger than me but at six feet, four inches in height was far from "little." I thought his height and rock concert experience might come in handy.

On October 20, 2001, as we walked from the parking garage to MSG the streets were quiet. It seemed all wrong. I remember thinking, *This is New York City on a Saturday night—quiet isn't normal.*

But the quiet gave way to loud as we entered MSG.

Our seats were a quarter of the way up the arena and slightly to the side of the stage. From where we were sitting, we not only had a great view of the stage, we could glimpse the backstage as well.

Thankfully, Fran brought earplugs for all of us.

The concert opened with David Bowie on stage. There were many amazing performers. Paul McCartney, Billy Joel, Elton John, James Taylor, and Backstreet Boys to name a few. Some performers I didn't know so I asked

"Meghan, who's this?"

"Five for Fighting," she replied.

I nodded.

A little later, Emily asked me, "Mom, who's this?"

"The Who."

"Who?"

"The Who."

It was like an Abbott and Costello routine. We dissolved into laughter. It felt good to laugh.

The firefighters made sure my daughters had a good time. Part way through the concert they asked permission to escort Emily and Meghan to the front row, so they could see Destiny's Child up close and personal.

There were short films by Woody Allen and Martin Scorsese. Different celebrities made appearances to offer encouragement. Harrison Ford was just as handsome in person as in the movies. Adam Sandler offered some funny moments as "Opera Man."

It was a loud but enjoyable evening.

Until the end.

The atmosphere totally changed when former President Bill Clinton came on stage. Boos. Curses. People, remembering an October 2000 attack on the USS Cole that had gone unchallenged, began yelling, "Remember the Cole! Remember the Cole!"

My brother and FDNY escorts stepped in closer to my daughters, my sister-in-law, and myself.

It was scary.

I found myself thinking of the roar of the crowds surrounding Jesus and the shouts of "Crucify Him!"

Looking back, I believe those moments escalated due to raw emotion (intensified by too much beer and lack of sleep).

It was a month and nine days after we had been attacked.

Healing was a long way away for all of us.

*   *   *

At the beginning of November, a large manila envelope arrived in the mail. The return address was the Medical Examiner's Office.

I opened every other piece of mail first. Eventually I couldn't put it off any longer.

I took a deep breath, exhaled, and whispered *Lord help me* as I opened it.

I carefully lifted out of the envelope ten copies of Bruce's death certificate.

The certificates were dated October 30, 2001. At first, I thought *I am not going to read this. Just stick them back in the envelope and file it somewhere safe.*

Then I began to read.

Basic information.

Name: Richard Bruce Van Hine.

Age: 49.

Location: World Trade Center.

Okay, that's all correct.

Glancing down the page I saw it:

Manner of death: Homicide.

I felt my breath catch.

I hadn't expected that. Actually, I don't know what I had expected.

Regardless, it was the truth.

* * *

In one of our weekly phone conversations, my mother-in-law sheepishly asked, "What's happening for Thanksgiving?"

Before answering I thought about the system Bruce and I had established years before. We typically spend odd-numbered years with the Van Hine extended family, and even numbered years with the Clarks.

2001 was an odd year.

"It's a Van Hine year. We were planning on coming to you."

My mother-in-law definitely had the gift of hospitality. She was a wonderful cook and hostess, and she had the amazing ability of finding those who needed a place to celebrate. Her table on holidays and many Sundays was surrounded by family, friends, and friends of friends.

I worried that there might be a houseful of people for Thanksgiving. I wasn't sure if I was up for that. But thankfully, she only had invited three of her lady friends. And for some reason (that I can't even articulate) they reminded me of the three fairies in *Sleeping Beauty*—Flora, Fauna, and Merryweather. Keeping that image in my head all day brought a smile to my face.

That evening I found a quiet place and moment for myself and wrote a letter to Bruce.

My dearest Bruce,

If anyone would have told me that by Thanksgiving, I would have been a widow for 10 weeks I wouldn't have believed them. You have been with the Lord since September 11. It seems like an eternity and like an instant. Time has no relation to anything as it once did. The days go by quickly, but they drag into weeks.

On that dreadful day the girls were afraid. They asked a lot of questions.

"Where's Daddy"

"Is he going to be all right?"

I told them you were doing your job. I didn't know where you were, but I knew that God was with you.

And then I told them, "I do know God is in control. And don't forget that God loves Daddy even more than we do."

They wanted to know what would happen if you died.

I told them you would go to heaven, and that we needed to trust God.

Then I asked them if someone we loved came to know Jesus through us losing you, would it be worth it? They said yes.

Then I switched that up a little and asked if *anyone* came to know Jesus because of us losing you, would it be worth it.

Again, they replied yes.

We counted the cost as we knew you would've wanted us to.

But that didn't mean the cost was easy to bear.

* * *

Throughout the month of December, as exhausting as my daily commute could be, I appreciated the silence on days I drove to or from work alone.

On other days, I was accompanied by Meghan and Emily, and those drives were precious as well. The drive provided a time to chat with no distractions. For nearly an hour, I was their captive audience, or they were mine.

One day I told them, "A parent asked me today, 'What are you doing *about* Christmas?' At first, I thought she was asking what are we doing *for* Christmas, but then I realized she was asking whether we are celebrating Christmas at all."

"What did you say?" asked Meghan.

"I said no matter what, Jesus was born and that is always worth celebrating."

"What *are* we doing?" inquired Emily.

"Well, on Sunday, Herb is going to take us to pick up a tree. Then we can decorate. We also have some interesting invitations, plus Cousin Jeremy's wedding is right after Christmas." I paused, then added, "But I've been meaning to ask you both about this. I want us to think about what we want to keep the same and what we want to change."

"What do you think about us doing 'Dad' gifts?" said Meghan.

"You mean the kind of gifts Dad would have bought each of us?" chuckled Emily. "Like his yearly gift to Mom of panty hose?"

"Exactly! Or the tool belt he gave you, or the tackle box he bought for me."

"That would be fun! I can buy a 'Dad' gift to you and Mom."

"And me and Mom can do the same."

"So, we'll each get two presents that remind us of Dad." Emily did the math.

"I like that idea." I added. "Oh, before I forget, the firehouse party is next Sunday."

Every year, Squad 41 hosted a lovely low–key event. It was an opportunity for the adults and teens to catch up as the younger kids climbed on the firetruck or explored the second floor to see where their daddies slept while on duty.

But that December, the party was morphing into something entirely different.

Charlie called ahead of time to warn me the party would be filmed by the TV show *EXTRA* as a way to bring attention to the Squad 41 Heroes Fund. In fact, celebrities would be dropping by for meet and greets.

On the day of the party, when Emily, Meghan, and I arrived, things felt normal—at first.

In the garage bay where the rig usually sat, long tables were laden with trays of delicious food prepared by the firefighters. Food and beverage choices were plentiful but—true to tradition—there wasn't a napkin in sight. It was a running joke. Every year, one of the wives would usually ask, "Hey, where are the napkins?" after which a roll of paper towels would eventually find its way onto the table.

But that's where all sense of "normal" came to screeching halt.

"Would you girls like to meet David Hasselhoff?" asked Eddie, the firefighter responsible for setting up *EXTRA*'s participation in this event.

"Sure," replied Emily and Meghan.

David Hasselhoff was taller than I thought he would be. He spent a long time talking to Emily and Meghan, asking questions about their dad, and how they were doing. He gave them autographed photos and his latest Christmas CD. He confessed to them he was a big hit in Germany.

A television crew wandered around dragging long electrical cords behind them as they filmed everyone and everything.

In the course of the day, others stopped by, including a few Broadway performers, some actors from *The Sopranos*, Miss Universe, Glenn Close, Mary Wilson from the Supremes, and Ginger from *Gilligan's Island*.

The girls and I tried to act nonchalant as we met and spoke to people we had previously only seen on television or in the movies.

At one point during the party, I was interviewed by a reporter for the TV station. He asked, "How are you coping?"

"I'm not coping," I responded, "I am hoping in Jesus."

By late afternoon, there was a loud thud on the roof. A firefighter yelled, "I think Santa is here."

Another familiar tradition. We rushed outside and watched as Santa rappelled down the side of the building with a large bag full of gifts for the kiddos, just as we had done for many years—minus the TV crews and celebrities, of course.

On the drive home from the firehouse, I was thinking about the interview with the reporter and said to Emily and Meghan, "I bet the soundbite will be 'I'm not coping.' Oh, well."

My next thought was, *How strange that I'm thinking about soundbites!*

A few days later the Squad 41 Christmas Party aired on *EXTRA*. After watching Emily and Meghan chatting with David Hasselhoff, we watched my interview. As a bonus, we received a copy of all the footage shot that day. I was surprised by the many hours of video that had been shot in order to produce a six-minute TV segment.

The 2001 holiday season brought invitations to attend the Rockefeller Tree Lightning, a party at Gracie Mansion, and the FDNY Widow and Children's Christmas Party to name a few larger-than-life opportunities.

Each event was amazing, but all these opportunities were bittersweet. Many times, I caught myself thinking, *Bruce would've loved this*, or *Wait until I tell Bruce about this*.

The FDNY Widow and Children's Holiday Party was one such event. The party was held at the newly opened Times Square Toys R Us, which on this particular Sunday morning was only open to beneficiaries and their guests. A full-sized Ferris wheel was the centerpiece of the store. Costumed characters and various athletes greeted us on the way to tables of delicious treats. It was a delightful event.

At the end of this event, Emily, Meghan, and I were each handed a large red mesh shopping bag full of gifts. Imprinted on each bag were the words *Toys R Us Times Square—For use in store only*. Walking out of the store carrying those bags, I hoped no one would think I had shoplifted! (And my fears weren't entirely unfounded, sometimes when I've used them since, they have indeed evoked some interesting conversations!)

As we walked to the car after the Toys 'R Us event, Emily said, "Mom, some of those other kids are so young they will never remember their dads."

"I noticed that, too."

"At least Meghan and I are old enough to have memories of Daddy."

Meghan nodded in agreement.

I was silent. There was nothing more to say.

8

TRICKY DAYS

I love decorating for Christmas. In recent years Meghan has commented that our house always looked like Christmas threw up. I took that as a compliment.

In the weeks leading up to Christmas 2001, I decorated the house in very much the same way I had in the past which left memories of Bruce sprinkled throughout.

One evening as I placed the handmade wooden reindeer with charred antlers on the fireplace hearth, a memory from years ago popped into my mind.

Bruce had been tending the fire as I'd walked into the room. I had noticed right away that the reindeer on the hearth was missing its antlers.

"Where are his antlers?" I'd asked. "One of my students gave me that. Her dad made it."

Bruce had gotten a strange look on his face. "Oops!"

He'd promptly put on his fireproof gloves, reached into the flames, and retrieved the antlers. Blowing out the embers, he'd said, "No problem. They'll be fine."

I'd shaken my head.

Just before Christmas a package arrived postmarked from Oklahoma. The sender was a new friend who had first contacted me a month earlier. The package contained many handmade items: a small goose–feathered tree, origami folded stars, old Christmas cards made into tiny boxes, and two small cardboard houses for my daughters with a twenty–dollar bill tucked inside each one.

But what made the whole thing so memorable was the way she signed the note. She had signed it: *A concerned Grama in Oklahoma.*

As soon as I saw her words, I teared up. It felt like a hug through time. I knew it was a gift to me, a nod from God.

Later, she would tell me that she'd felt a strong urge to sign the note that way, even though she didn't know why. In fact, she admitted, she'd felt ridiculous doing it. But she was convinced she was supposed to write those words.

When I explained that my grandparents, in heaven now for many years, were from Oklahoma, it suddenly made sense to her.

She knew that she had, indeed, heard from God.

I knew it, too.

Emily, Meghan, and I skipped Christmas Eve service at church. Instead, we hunkered down at home and watched a Christmas movie followed by our traditional Christmas eve dinner of our favorite appetizers: shrimp, veggie platter, cheese and crackers, mozzarella sticks, and Fritos with onion dip.

Christmas Eve didn't feel that different than usual.

But Christmas morning did.

I made a tray of tea, then preheated the oven for French bread toast, just as I'd done on Christmas morning for many years.

As I turned from the oven, I glanced in the direction of the living room and remembered when the girls were younger.

Every Christmas morning, the doorway to the living room had been blocked by red ribbon—along with a note from Santa instructing the girls not to open any gifts until Daddy got home. They would open their stockings and make gingerbread houses as they waited for Daddy to be off duty.

Still standing at the oven, memories in my eyes, I thought to myself, *But he's not on duty this morning. He's not coming home.*

I picked up the tray of tea and headed into the living room.

We sat on the living room floor to exchange our Dad gifts, that special something Dad would have bought.

We cried together.

We hugged each other.

We prayed together.

We each took a deep breath.

And then we opened our other gifts.

Christmas 2001 brought more gifts under our tree than we had ever seen. A Sunday School class in Tennessee adopted us and sent gifts: a Tennessee shaped cutting board, sweatshirts, and notes from members of their youth group to Emily and Meghan were included. A little ceramic firehouse labeled Squad 41 came with a check. For me, there was a pair of leopard pajamas that weren't my style but quickly became my favorite.

By mid-afternoon we headed to my folks' house for Christmas dinner.

Christmas had been a *tricky day.* That's what Emily, Meghan, and I had begun calling those days filled with both celebrating and grieving. They were days of gratefulness and emptiness. Days to cherish rituals while establishing new traditions.

Tricky days.

* * *

Right after Christmas, Emily, Meghan, and I flew to Chicago for the wedding of Bruce's youngest nephew. Spending time with the Van Hine side of the family offered a welcome diversion from our *new* normal, as well as a chance to share stories and make memories.

This was the second Bower wedding in 2001. The first had been the wedding of Bruce's niece in August.

When the first wedding had been announced, Bruce and I had agreed we couldn't really afford for him to go. At the same time, I felt strongly that Bruce needed to be at that wedding. In fact, I knew he was supposed to go and escort his mom.

And so, we found a way to make that happen.

It is strange how there are things you feel strongly about, and you don't understand why until later. More than one person at the December wedding mentioned meeting Bruce at the August wedding, and how the September 11 attacks had a deeper meaning because they had met an FDNY firefighter. Just as importantly, Bruce's presence at that August wedding allowed him special time with his mom, sister, and her family.

While the girls and I were in Chicago for the second wedding, a *New York Times* reporter, Gretchen Morgenson, called to interview me for Bruce's Portrait of Grief in a *New York Times* series.

We spoke late one night by phone as Emily and Meghan slept nearby.

Gretchen said, "Tell me about Bruce."

I spoke of his journey to become a firefighter and his love of the outdoors. I explained how excited he had been in early September when he had completed the last hike needed to be able to boast that he had hiked the complete Appalachian Trail from New Jersey to Connecticut. He had hiked it one section at a time just doing day hikes over the course of a few years, but he had done it.

"What is a prized memory that you have?" Gretchen asked.

"We took a five–week camping trip a few years ago." I replied. "We called it our National Parks Tour. We visited the Badlands, Yellowstone, Grand Tetons, Rocky Mountain National Park." I chuckled. "It did get a little tense a times—with four people and a dog in a pop-up—but it was great."

Her piece appeared on December 31, 2001, as part of the series "A Nation Challenged: Portraits of Grief: The Victims."

Thinking about moments like these—Bruce escorting his mom to a family wedding, Bruce's hiking accomplishment, our family camping trips—reminds me of a quote by (of all people!) Dr. Seuss.

He once wrote, "Sometimes you never know the value of a moment until it is a memory."

So true.

* * *

A month later, back at home, I opened the door to the fellowship hall with trepidation. What had I gotten myself into?

It was a meeting of an FDNY widows' support group. I had never been a part of a therapy group before; I was skeptical that it had anything to offer me.

As I entered, I saw about a dozen women ranging in age from their twenties to their sixties sitting in a circle. The leader introduced herself and opened the discussion.

One woman mentioned she had contacted a psychic.

Oh, great! I knew I shouldn't have come.

Another woman shared an insight she had received from a widow friend: "Don't read romance novels."

We all chuckled.

Someone else added another tidbit of wisdom: "And if you need something done, don't put it off. Pay someone to do it or learn to do it yourself."

That was advice I could use.

When I left the meeting, I thought to myself, *Maybe I will return again in two weeks.*

And I did.

Attending the gatherings helped me realize several things.

For starters, I had less of a learning curve than some of the other widows. I had always taken care of the bills, so that wasn't an adjustment. But Bruce had always taken care of the garbage, oil changes, home maintenance, and lawn care, so those areas presented a steep learning curve.

I also realized that, while we all had extensive support from the brotherhood of firefighters, I had something more. Bruce had always said "If I die in the line of duty, you will be taken care of," and that was proving true for me as well as for the other widows of firefighters. But I had something special in the support from family, friends, and my church that many of the other women didn't have.

Attending the meetings provided yet another level of support. I came to appreciate the feelings I could express to that group of women that I didn't feel I could say anywhere else without a lot of explanation. To this day, two of the women from that support group are still cherished friends and confidants.

In time, I began to feel that I was walking on solid ground. Everyday life had a rhythm to it. The invitations to special events weren't as constant. We were finding balance.

And then a letter from the medical examiner's office arrived that made me feel like I was standing in a rocking boat.

The letter informed me that the medical examiner's office didn't have DNA samples for Bruce.

As I read the letter, my thoughts came fast and furious:

Yes, you do.

Emily and I had our cheeks swabbed,

I gave you his toothbrush and dirty t-shirt. Squad 41 gave you items from Bruce's locker. I can't replace those items.

This is a mistake.

I read the next sentence of the letter with my mouth hanging open: "The following items may contain DNA: toothbrush, comb, clothing, *chewed gum.*"

CHEWED GUM?

Is this a joke?

Like, after four months, I have a piece of his chewed gum lying around.

As if this is junior high and it's stuck under a desk somewhere.

Are you freakin' kidding me?

I was so upset by the insensitivity of suggesting *chewed gum* that I spent the rest of my evening grumbling about the entire situation.

But even more upsetting was the thought that, after all this time, they had no record of his DNA—which meant that remains could not be positively identified.

I thought this had been taken care of months ago. I couldn't believe the items I had provided had been lost or discarded somehow. I couldn't go backwards. I just couldn't.

The next morning, I dialed the medical examiner's office. As I waited for someone to answer the phone, I felt my jaw clench and my body tense. *Stay calm.*

"Medical examiner's office," someone answered. It sounded like a young man.

"Good morning. My name is Ann Van Hine. My husband was one of the firefighters killed on September 11."

"Sorry for your loss. How can I help you?"

"Yesterday, I received a letter saying you don't have items to test for Bruce's DNA," I explained in a rather firm tone. "Well, you do." In an even sterner voice I added, "Suggesting that chewed gum is good for DNA testing is beyond insensitive. My husband died four months ago—do you really think I have a piece of his chewed gum lying around?"

"No, ma'am, I don't. That is a form letter."

"I know it is a form letter, but it wasn't appropriate. Come up with a new form. I can guarantee you that other September 11 family members are going to go even more ballistic than I just did. Please. Think. Think about what you're sending before you send it!"

"Ma'am, if you give me your husband's full name, I can check our record."

"Thank you."

He found nothing under Bruce's name. I assured him I had definitely submitted DNA. He suggested calling the lab where Emily and I had our cheeks swabbed.

Instead, I called Christine and asked her to look into what had happened.

After a few telephone calls, Christine learned that in the aftermath of the attacks, more than one agency had established a database of information. A different agency did, indeed, have Bruce's DNA, which we were able to get transferred to the medical examiner's office.

* * *

My birthday took place in February. I have often joked that Bruce never really knew the date of my birthday. He just knew it was the day before Valentine's Day. So as those Valentine's Day ads started appearing on television or on the radio, he knew my birthday was around the corner.

On Valentine's Day 2002, I received a dozen red roses from Squad 41. I loved the gesture. I laughed because Bruce never gave me roses on Valentine's Day—they were just too expensive. Bruce bought me flowers on other days but no flowers on Valentine's Day. The roses from Squad 41 were a first.

A few days later, a telephone call brought an exciting opportunity.

"Hi, Ann. It's Steve from Squad 41."

"Hi, Steve."

"We thought you and the girls might be interested in a trip to France. The trip is sponsored by the Paris Fire Department."

"Wow!"

"Actually, we thought of you because you have culture."

Steve explained that we would be staying with a French firefighter's family and at least one member of the family could speak some English. The French I remembered from four years of classes in high school was limited to *merci, au revoir,* and *où est la bibliothèque,* which means "Where is the library?"

I wasn't really sure what the comment "you have culture" meant, but this seemed like an awesome experience.

The Monday before we left for our trip to France, my phone rang.

I'll be honest, the ring of the phone or a blinking light on the answering machine usually evoked a gut reaction of *Now what?* To just have a normal day—or rather, a "new" normal day—with no bad news or surprises was still my hope. But this wasn't going be that day.

The phone continued ringing. Thankfully, I answered it in my bedroom.

"Hi, Ann, This is Eddie from Squad 41."

"Hi, Eddie. What's happening?"

"We've found some tools at the site labeled Squad 41."

"Oh."

"We are pretty sure we will be finding bodies." He paused. "There's a reporter from Chicago who would like to interview you. You've spoken to him in the past."

"Sure. And, Eddie, thanks for letting me know about the tools."

"Talk to you soon."

I didn't mention anything to Emily and Meghan about the tools. I wasn't sure what would come of it, or what it meant in the whole scheme of things.

9

NEW NORMAL, TAKE 3

∞

We were all packed for our late Saturday afternoon flight to Paris. My dad would be driving us to the JFK airport.

Late Friday night the telephone rang. Jarred out of deep sleep, I grabbed for the receiver. "Hello?"

"Ann, it's Charlie. They found Bruce's body." He hesitated. "I think I already know the answer to this question, but I have to ask. Do you want to come and see him carried out? If so, we would have four hours to get you to the site. We would come and pick you up."

I sat up as thoughts swirled around in my head.

I can't leave the house in the middle of night.

Who will stay with the girls?

I can't do this.

Silence on both ends of the phone.

"Ann?"

"I can't do it."

"That's okay. I thought that would be your answer. Look, I still want you to go to Paris. Positive identification could take six weeks, so go to France. I will talk to you when you get back."

"Okay. Charlie, thank you. Please tell the others thank you."

I didn't say anything right away to anyone about Bruce's body being found.

This is my life. It's my loss. I want to process it before I have to share it.

Emily, Meghan, and I boarded the flight to Paris at JFK airport.

As we were waiting for the plane to begin the taxi for takeoff, a three-year-old in the seat ahead of ours peeked over the seat and asked Emily:

"Where are you going?"

"Paris."

"Me, too!"

The girl's mother turned around and we introduced ourselves. Another widow, Laurie was traveling with her three young daughters as part of the same FDNY group. Her husband had been a firefighter in Rescue 5 in Staten Island.

We instantly bonded. She seemed so. . . normal. A mom, just like me, traveling with her daughters. Our bond was rooted in tragedy, but we didn't focus on that. It was just nice to have a met a new friend.

We arrived in Paris early in the morning to VIP treatment, lovely but unexpected. We boarded a large bus heading to the Fire Academy where we would meet the host families in whose homes we would be staying.

On the way there, we toured the streets of Paris and got a quick glance of the city waking up for the day.

As the bus pulled into the parking lot of the Fire Academy, we heard a band and saw American and French flags being flown. Onlookers, firefighters, and camera crews milled about.

Upon entering the building, we were handed a portfolio that had a photo of our host family. The host family had a photo of us. It was strange to see people wandering around holding up photos trying to make a connection.

Smiles, giggles, head shakes eventually ended with a match.

We sat with our host family and ate breakfast. Actually, we ate breakfast three times that morning—on the plane, in the VIP lounge at the Charles de Gaulle Airport, and then at the Fire Academy.

We eventually realized Emily had been assigned to a different host family. So many French firefighter families had wanted to host FDNY families, they had placed the older teens in separate homes. The intention was fine, but I felt that separating the teens from their mothers in this situation wasn't a good idea.

Meghan and I moved into the guest room in the home of our host family. The husband was retired Paris Fire Department and spoke no English. The wife knew how to say, "Would you like this or this?" as she pointed to different items. Their college-age daughter spoke English quite well. Still, we relied a lot on a French/English dictionary, hand gestures, smiles, and a sense of humor to help with communication.

Emily, however, was having a very different experience. In her host family, a teenage daughter spoke English but for some reason—some kind of power play or immaturity or shyness—she refused to speak to Emily in English. The girl's mother and father were very gracious and tried to remedy the situation, but poor Emily was stuck in the middle.

Within a couple days we managed to get Emily moved in with us without causing an international incident.

Over the next two days, we toured the countryside visiting local sights, farms, and historical homes.

On Tuesday morning the host family dropped us off to catch the tour bus to Disneyland Paris. We were to have a private tour guide and VIP access to rides and attractions.

As we boarded the bus, we spotted Laurie and her girls and eagerly reconnected. Laurie and I sat together while the five girls chatted in seats around us.

Laurie and I chatted about our experiences so far in Paris.

During a lull in the conversation, I felt the weight of the words I had yet to speak to a soul.

Words I had been living with for three days.

I turned to Laurie and said, "They found my husband's body."

To this day, I don't remember what she said in response. What could she say?

What I do remember is a sense of relief to finally have spoken the unspeakable. I also remember a sense of the surreal.

The twin towers had fallen six months ago, and we were still getting heart–wrenching news. The landscape of my life was still changing.

Would this never end?

The rest of the week was a blur of private tours, banquets, and sightseeing.

Friday was reserved for the sights of Paris. Emily and I decided not to go to the top of the Eiffel Tower, but Meghan did venture to the top with a few of the firefighters. She took some photos I am glad I didn't see her take as I am pretty sure she was leaning too far over the side of the railing.

The last big event was a Friday evening dinner cruise on the River Seine with all kinds of bigwigs in the Paris Fire Department. They had champagne bottled with a special Paris FD and FDNY label. We were given a bottle to take home.

It had become a joke during the week that the only French phrase I knew was *Ou est la bibliotheque?* At one point on the dinner cruise a couple of firefighters came to our table and pointed out the window as we passed the Paris library.

"Ann, *la bibliotheque!*"

Everyone laughed.

Friday night was spent at the airport hotel repacking our suitcases to fit many beautiful gifts not only from the Paris FD but our host family as well.

As we flew home, I told the girls Eddie had called to tell me they'd found tools indicating where firefighters from Squad 41 had been working.

I didn't mention that Bruce's body had also been found.

When we got home, the answering machine was blinking.

I listened to the first message, which was from Bruce's cousin asking about funeral details. The second message was from a friend stating he was available to be a pallbearer.

What?

How does everyone know?

What is happening?

The last message was from Charlie, asking me to contact him when I had a minute. I called him and left a message.

Easter Sunday morning Charlie called back.

"The DNA results came back. They have officially identified Bruce's body. Can someone come to your house Monday evening to give you the official notification?"

"That's not necessary. I work on Mondays."

"Just tell me what time is good for you."

"Eight p.m."

Truth is, while I was grateful they had found Bruce's body, I also felt angry and frustrated. The results were supposed to have taken *weeks*, not days—and word had gotten out before I'd been able to prepare Emily and Meghan, or even tell any family members or close friends.

Now my hand had been forced. I had to tell my girls that their daddy's body had been found and identified.

And on Easter morning, no less.

To be honest we never thought there would be a body. How could I tell them there was indeed a body—on a day when we were celebrating the absence of a body? Not Bruce's, of course, but Christ's. It took years for me to fully grasp the implications of the timing. Eventually I came to see it as beautiful. You see, whether Bruce's body was found or not, my hope was built on the story of Jesus' resurrection.

On that Sunday, before heading to my folks' house for Easter dinner, I told Emily and Meghan I had something important to share with them.

We sat around the kitchen table.

"Just before we left for France," I said, "Charlie called and told me they thought they had found Daddy's body." I paused. "Charlie also said it could take six weeks to identify him so that's why I didn't say anything. But now they have identified him."

My daughters sat in stunned silence.

"The FDNY will come tomorrow evening," I added, "to give us the official notification, but some way or the other the news has gotten out. Some people already know."

"Wow. I didn't think they would find his body," Emily said. "But at least now I don't have to wonder if Daddy is wandering around with amnesia."

I never knew she was thinking that.

Meghan added, "I've had no control in any of this—but telling my friends his body was found was something I should've had some control over. Not anyone else."

"You're right. I'm sorry. I will try to find out how this happened."

We each finished getting ready to leave, lost in our own thoughts. The ride to my parents' house was quiet.

Before dinner, I told my family that Bruce's body had been found and identified.

For the first time in my life, I saw my dad cry.

At the studio on Monday, I asked Carol if she would come to the house and be with me for the official notification. She did. Tony came, too.

At 8 p.m. on Monday, April 1, Firefighter Richie Ting, in full dress uniform, informed me on behalf of the FDNY that Bruce's body had been identified.

Emily and Meghan chose to stay in their rooms until Richie, Carol, and Tony had left.

Then we discussed what Daddy would have wanted.

"He wanted to be cremated," Meghan said.

I knew that.

"We already did a service. We don't want to do that again," Emily said, and Meghan agreed with her.

"It is your choice. I feel we have done what was expected of us. The rest of this is totally up to the two of you."

A few days later on my morning off, I went to the local funeral parlor to make the arrangements for cremation.

Later, when I picked Emily up from school, she said, "I want to go with you to the funeral parlor."

"Em, I went this morning."

"Who went with you?"

"I went alone."

"What? you shouldn't have had to do that alone."

"Em, Auntie Carol, Aunt Christine, or numerous other people would have come with me if I had asked, but I had to do it alone." I paused. "Actually, they did volunteer to come but this was a job just for me. I had to do this alone."

"But Mom."

"Emily, no seventeen-year-old should have to make burial arrangements for their father. I couldn't have done it if you were there."

Just as we were moving forward, I felt we were pushed back. I was putting out fires. I questioned my decision to postpone telling anyone his body was found.

I even started thinking how bad it would have looked if I'd told everyone before I'd left. What would people have thought?

They find his body and off she goes to Paris.

But I knew my motivation was to avoid undue stress. I didn't want people calling for six weeks asking if the body had been identified yet. I didn't want the girls upset every time the phone rang.

Yet so many people were hurt that I hadn't told them right away.

I had no words except, "You know me. It wasn't intentional."

I informed family and friends there would not be a second service. Bruce's body would be cremated, and Emily and Meghan would decide what would happen to his ashes.

People didn't necessarily understand or agree with my decision to not have another service, but resolve drove me forward. Only Emily and Meghan's choices mattered.

When I explained to my mother-in-law our plans, she was very concerned about Bruce's ashes. She mentioned that her friend had kept her husband's ashes on the shelf in her closet for years. I promised her I would never stick Bruce on the shelf in the closet.

Emily and Meghan had ideas as to where they wanted to scatter Daddy's ashes: on the Appalachian Trail or in the ocean (Bruce loved scuba diving).

But we agreed there was no rush.

No "right thing" to do.

Daddy was safely with God, where he has been ever since September 11.

His ashes are in a beautiful wooden box that sits in my bedside table.

In May 2002, I received Bruce's revised death certificate.

It lists the manner of death as homicide.

It also lists the immediate cause of death as blunt head trauma.

When I read that, I thought about the fact that an entire building had collapsed on him.

Blunt head trauma seemed like an understatement.

Bruce, Ann, Emily, and Meghan at Bruce's FDNY graduation. 1990

Bruce and Charlie spending night on Appalachian Trial. August 2001

Bruce and Meghan at her eighth-grade graduation. June 2001

Bruce in his turnout gear.

*Soaring Crane in
Kaisezan Park,
Koriyama, Japan*

*Plaque on
Soaring Crane*

Soaring Crane

This origami crane is made from steel recovered from the World Trade Center site in New York. It is a gift of hope from the September 11th Families' Association and 9/11 Tribute Center. We extend compassion to the people who lived through the tragic earthquake of March 11, 2011. We wish you strength and courage as you move forward to rebuild your lives and communities. We send special wishes to the children for peace.

Last Column in Foundation Hall, National September 11th Memorial Museum

Ann's official photo at NASDAQ

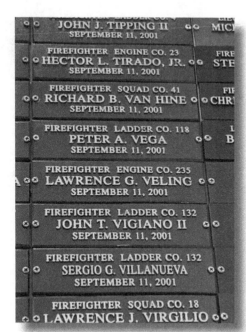

FIREFIGHTER ENGINE CO. 23
HECTOR L. TIRADO, JR.
SEPTEMBER 11, 2001

FIREFIGHTER SQUAD CO. 41
RICHARD B. VAN HINE
SEPTEMBER 11, 2001

FIREFIGHTER LADDER CO. 118
PETER A. VEGA
SEPTEMBER 11, 2001

FIREFIGHTER ENGINE CO. 235
LAWRENCE G. VELING
SEPTEMBER 11, 2001

FIREFIGHTER LADDER CO. 132
JOHN T. VIGIANO II
SEPTEMBER 11, 2001

FIREFIGHTER LADDER CO. 132
SERGIO G. VILLANUEVA
SEPTEMBER 11, 2001

FIREFIGHTER SQUAD CO. 18
LAWRENCE J. VIRGILIO

Bruce's name on the Line of Duty Deaths plaque

FDNY Headquarters – Line-of Duty Deaths

Bruce's name on FDNY 9/11 memorial

Ann leading a 9/11 Tribute Museum tour. Explaining FDNY 9/11 memorial

Bruce's name on the National September 11th Memorial Plaza. Yellow roses are placed on the memorial on Veteran's Day. Bruce served in the Navy.

The new One World Trade Center

10

THE FIRST ANNIVERSARY

∞

As I stood backstage watching my youngest students dance, I felt Bruce's absence more profoundly than I had anticipated.

The annual dance recital was an event that took a year in planning—theme, music, choreography, costumes, tickets, programs, scenery, ushers, classroom attendants—teaching all the dances to my students.

But no matter how well-organized Carol and I were, anything could happen—and often did! Which is why, every year, Bruce took the day off work and made sure he was available to help any way he could.

He carried in gym mats, boxes of hats, and scenery supplies. He drove to Radio Shack to pick up missing cords, or to the deli to pick up lunch. He tracked down the custodian to unlock classrooms, and helped families get their wheelchair–bound loved ones into the building.

He didn't correct anyone when they called him Mr. Clark.

Once the show began, he would stand off stage, out of the way but attentive to whatever I needed. Sometimes he wandered out front to watch Emily and Meghan dance, or to check if the sound level was good.

Throughout the ninety–minute performance, he cheered us all on.

When it was over, he gave me a kiss on the forehead and said, "Good show, Miss Ann."

I didn't realize what a gift all that had been until his spot off stage stood empty.

His absence was profoundly felt again a few days later at Emily's high school graduation. Knowing how greatly his loss would be felt on that day, a few firefighters from Squad 41 attended Emily's graduation in full dress uniform and held up a large banner that read "Congratulations Emily!"

* * *

"Mrs. Van Hine, this is the mayor's office calling. Please hold for the mayor."

A moment later, the Mayor of New York City came on the line. "Mrs. Van Hine, I want to express my condolences on behalf of the City of New York."

"Thank you so much for calling. I appreciate you taking the time. I know you must be very busy and had many people to call."

"Actually, I am almost done with the list."

Wait, what?

When I relayed the conversation to my dad, he commented, "The anniversary is approaching, and he wants to be able to say he called all the victim's families."

To be honest, the comment left me stunned. Eventually I realized it was an extraordinary time, and maybe the *almost done* comment was an unguarded moment. Or perhaps it showcased the difference between a businessman and a politician.

Our invitation to attend NYC's first September 11 memorial service arrived mid- summer. As the date loomed on the horizon, I felt uneasy. Was there an appropriate thing to do? What were the expectations?

In a conversation with Carol, she said, "Do what you want to do."

Those six little words gave me the freedom I needed. It lifted the burden of expectations—real or imagined.

Emily, Meghan, and I decided not to go to the memorial service at all.

We agreed that, on the anniversary of the attack, we wanted to be together, just the three of us—just as we had been on September 11, 2001. We had always felt that the world—family, friends, firefighters—had arrived on September 12, 2001. But the hours immediately following the attacks had belonged to us.

* * *

"Mom, do you think it would be weird if I hung a photo of Daddy on my locker at school?"

"Meghan, that sounds lovely. Which photo?"

"I think the one in his turnout gear, and maybe I will add a Bible verse or something."

"That sounds like a good idea."

Meghan hung a single 8.5 by 11–inch sheet of paper that included the photo of her dad and Revelation 7:15–17 Scripture verse.

"Therefore, they are before the throne of God and serve him day and night in his temple; and he who sits on the throne will spread his tent over them. Never again will they hunger; never again will they thirst. The sun will not beat upon them, nor any scorching heat. For the Lamb at the center of the throne will be their shepherd; he will lead them to springs of living water. And God will wipe away every tear from their eyes."

Since Emily had already started her freshman year of college, Meghan and I drove to Massachusetts the night of September 10 and stayed in a local hotel.

The morning of September 11, 2002, we arrived on campus in time to meet Emily for the chapel service.

The guest speaker was Dr. Mucci—a friend, mentor, and the person I had, a year earlier, suggested to God was the one righteous person in NYC.

After chapel, the girls and I headed to the nearby Quincy Beach to share stories about Daddy and to pray. We then had coffee at Friendly's as I explained to the girls that I bought a composition notebook so we could record things we wished we could share with Bruce about events since his death.

I had titled the notebook *Things We Would Have Told You*, and on the first page, I had written:

Bruce—I bought this notebook so we could tell you things. Needless to say, I know this is really just a notebook and that we can't actually tell you these things, but I think the Lord allows you a peek at us every now and then. The truth is that we will have eternity to tell you all you have missed! We love you!! Ann, Emily, and Meghan.

Emily and Meghan mentioned things that happened in the year and I wrote them in the book. Five pages' worth.

September 11, 2002—thoughts written while sitting in Friendly's in Quincy, MA near ENC:
Emily looked beautiful for the prom. You would have thrown your body across the door to keep her home.

Meghan can't open her locker.

Emily learned to replace doorknobs.

Mom was on TV three times

We saw Bill Clinton get booed

Meghan was a counselor-in-training at camp

Emily goes to Monday Night Football when she's at college

We continued to write in that composition notebook every year on September 11 for the next four years, until 2006.

After an hour or so at Friendly's, we left and headed into Boston to visit Faneuil Hall, an outdoor/indoor market area. Emily's newfound knowledge of Boston's subway system came in handy.

But as we got to Faneuil Hall, we saw a stage, banners, crowds, and reporters—and realized they were holding a ceremony commemorating the first anniversary of September 11.

We shot each other a look that said, "Are you kidding me?" We had avoided the New York City ceremony to walk right into the ceremony in Boston!

Keep your head down. Don't stop. Don't talk. Don't cry.

Once we were past the cameras and reporters, we shook our heads in disbelief. We wandered through the shops, had lunch, and ended the day feeling that we had done the "right thing" by focusing on our family.

I will say that many friends and family members texted or called us throughout the day. And when Meghan returned to school on Friday, September 13, classmates, and teachers had covered the front of her locker with notes bearing words of encouragement.

We felt loved.

Bruce was remembered well.

With the first September 11 anniversary behind us, there was still a big memorial service at Madison Square Garden ahead of us.

The venue seats more than 20,000 people. However, with 343 FDNY firefighters, three WTC fire marshals and one Fire Patrol member all killed on September 11, 2001 being honored as well as nine other firefighters killed in the line of duty between November 2000 and October 2002, there was some question about whether the venue would be big enough.

Inside Madison Square Garden was a large stage where all the dignitaries sat. The honor families and their escorts sat on chairs arranged in front of the stage.

It was ice hockey season, and the chairs had been set up on a temporary plywood floor over the ice rink. My toes froze. To be honest it was a good distraction from the sorrowfulness of the event.

Around the arena hung cloth reproductions of the portraits Peter Maxx had painted of each fallen firefighter. (I eventually received the original painting.)

The ceremony began with the presenting of the colors followed by 356 firefighters carrying American flags. Those firefighters stood around the first tier of seats for the entire ceremony honoring those killed in the line of duty since November 2000.

Former Mayor Rudy Giuliani, current Mayor Michael Bloomberg, Fire Commissioner Nicholas Scoppetta, Chief of the Department Frank Cruthers all spoke, and Irish Tenor Ronan Tynan sang "You Raise Me Up."

The ceremony continued with a video featuring the names and photos of the fallen. After the last name was spoken, there was a standing ovation and thunderous applause like I had never experienced in my life. The applause grew in intensity as it went on and on. Cheers and whistling were added and every attempt from the platform to end it was futile. The firefighters needed to honor their fallen comrades, and they did. It was heartbreaking and awe-inspiring at the same time.

Once the applause ended the families were instructed to stand for the presentation of medals by their FDNY escorts.

Charlie, in full dress uniform including white gloves, presented me with a beautiful long wooden box engraved with the emblems of the FDNY and the three fire department unions. Inside the velvet-lined box were displayed Bruce's four medals—including a Supreme Sacrifice medal, a medal of valor from the Fire Department of the City of New York and a special September 11, 2001 medal of valor—on different colored ribbons. A plaque had been engraved with the words "Fire Fighter Richard B. Van Hine, Fire Department—City of New York, IAFF Local 94, September 11, 2001."

The ceremony ended with the Emerald Society Pipes and Drums marching in and playing "America the Beautiful" followed by Ronan Tynan singing "God Bless America." Everyone was asked to remain in their seats as the honor families were escorted out.

This was the FDNY at their best. Tradition—longstanding tradition that is foundational to all that the FDNY is and does—gave us all strength.

* * *

Thanksgiving 2002 was a Clark year. We gathered with my folks at Christine's house. It was a lovely time, but we also realized that second holidays can actually be harder than first. You aren't numb anymore. You can feel the loss.

Throughout 2002, I had spoken seventeen times, mostly at ladies' church groups but also at Emily's high school graduation, and the National Laymen's Retreat for the Church of the Nazarene in Nashville, Tennessee.

The invitation to speak at the National Laymen's Retreat had been a big one.

Meghan and I flew to Nashville, Tennessee in July 2002. Sitting behind the General Superintendents for the Church of the Nazarene in the conference area of the Gaylord Opryland Resort felt like I was running with the big kids. *Lord, are you sure about this?*

After I shared our experiences, I added, "This isn't really my story or even Bruce's story. It is God's story."

After the program, there was a reception for the speakers and the bigwigs in the penthouse. *Definitely running with the big kids now. What am I doing here?*

Everyone was very friendly and tried to make us feel comfortable. Eventually we sat down at a large table to eat our late–night snack.

The wife of one of the general superintendents said, "You mentioned you stopped by your studio. What kind of studio do you own? Is it an art studio?"

I wasn't sure if I wanted to laugh or cry at the question.

It seems like a simple question and it was asked with sincere interest, but in my head, I could hear my husband belly laughing and chanting "you go, girl."

Through the years, Bruce and I had chuckled on more than one occasion about me being *the dancer girl*—the nickname his parents used for me when we were first dating. His parents and even the Church of the Nazarene had a conservative view on dancing. Yes, I taught dance, but I was also Sunday school superintendent in my local church and children's ministries director for the Metro New York District. This proved to be an interesting juxtaposition for some people.

So, on this occasion, I took a deep breath and answered, "It is a dance studio. I teach little girls ballet." The response was warm and those gathered shared stories of their granddaughters' dance recitals.

As soon as Meghan and I were alone in the elevator heading to our room, we started laughing.

"Mom, I couldn't believe she asked you that. Daddy was laughing in heaven."

"Yes, he was."

Over the year, I learned that speaking at a scheduled appearance was one thing but speaking on the fly was another. My response to the question "Would you like to say a few words?" became "Yes," followed by a quick silent prayer: "Okay, Lord, what am I saying?"

Learning to trust God to give me His words was a new experience, but He faithfully supplied what I needed on every occasion.

In December of 2002, as I finished speaking at my last scheduled event, I thanked the Lord for all the opportunities I had to share Bruce's story. I thanked Him for allowing my words to help other people.

The Lord's response was He had allowed me to speak to keep me close to Him.

What I thought I was doing for others the Lord was doing for me.

11

THE WHITE HOUSE, A WEDDING, AND WALKING TOURS

∞

As the days became weeks and weeks became years, our *new* normal had a rhythm to it. I continued teaching dance, fulfilling my responsibilities as district children's ministries director, and enjoying time spent with family and friends. I lived in the same house and attended the same church that Bruce and I had for years.

My life was pretty much the same in terms of what I did each day, but I missed Bruce—his companionship, encouragement, and intimacy.

My mom duties were also changing as Emily and Meghan grew up. Emily was at college and dating a young man named Scott. Meghan would soon be off to college as well.

And each July without fail, an invitation to the New York City September 11 anniversary ceremony would arrive in the mail. There was a time when the anniversary felt like a large dark creature waiting to pounce on me. Over time I realized what I was fearing was a shadow.

Bruce dying in the line of duty couldn't happen again because it already happened on September 11, 2001. I came to understand that if I was looking at September 11, the sun/ Son were behind me, so the shadow was in front of me. But if I looked at the sun/Son, the shadow was behind me.

Walt Whitman expresses it this way: "Keep your face always toward the sunshine—and shadows will fall behind you." Good advice.

* * *

In September 2005 a special invitation started with an unlikely telephone call.

"Mrs. Van Hine? This is Eric from the Department of Justice calling on behalf of the White House."

I scribbled the word White House on a piece of paper and handed it to Emily. She started to ask questions. I wagged my finger meaning no. I concentrated on what was being said.

"The White House would like to invite you and your daughters to attend a ceremony. The president will present the Congressional Medal of Valor to the families of all first responders killed in the line of duty on September 11, 2001. Would you be interested in attending?"

"Yes, thank you."

"You will be receiving information in the mail as to how you can arrange travel at no expense to you. Will your daughters be traveling with you?"

"Yes, but the one just started college in Pennsylvania."

"We can fly her in."

"Actually, I can just drive and pick her up."

"When you receive the information just contact the travel office and sort out what works for you."

"Thank you."

Emily and I called Meghan.

"Guess what?"

* * *

Because Washington, DC was just a two–hour drive from Meghan's college, we decided to drive there instead of fly.

When we arrived in DC, we followed directions to an assigned meeting place where buses arrived to transport us to the White House.

An hour or so later the girls and I—along with two hundred other first responder family members—were seated in folding chairs on the south lawn of the White House. Risers filled with members of the press were behind us.

And, everywhere, men in suits roamed, talking into their sleeves.

"The ceremony doesn't start for another thirty minutes," I mentioned to the girls. "And it's hot sitting in the sun. Why don't we go for a little walk?"

"Sounds good," said Emily, fanning herself with one of the paper fans we'd been given along with programs.

We headed for shade, taking a tree–covered path that wound away from the White House.

"It's a little cooler here," I said.

Suddenly we were greeted by two men in tactical gear carrying big guns.

"Ma'am, can we help you?" said one of the men.

Emily, Meghan, and I shared a look that said *Oh, my goodness!*

"No, thank you," I quickly said. "We were just taking a little walk."

"I'm going to have to ask you to please return to your seats."

"Yes, of course. Sorry."

Back in our seats we chuckled about our misadventure.

"Who knew there were men in the bushes!" I laughed.

"This could only happen to us!" Meghan giggled. "Only we could come to the White House and stumble upon the guys with the big guns!"

Eventually the ceremony began. President George W. Bush and Attorney General Alberto Gonzalez spoke words of honor and remembrance.

As the president got ready to leave, many people moved forward to shake his and/or Mrs. Bush's hand. He spent time with those who approached him. While I took a few photos, I didn't go forward. I felt this event was about honoring Bruce, not meeting the president.

Around the perimeter of the lawn were tables labeled with letters of the alphabet, and next to each table stood a marine in dress uniform as well as a Department of Justice staff person. On the table were navy blue boxes containing the Congressional Medal of Valor as well as certificates in leather–bound presentation frames.

As we arrived at the table the staff person said, "Mrs. Van Hine, please accept this medal on behalf of a grateful nation." The marine handed me the box and saluted. It was humbling.

We were proud of Bruce and knew he would have said he was just doing his job.

After the ceremony we drove back to Pennsylvania and Emily spent the night with Meghan in her dorm room.

I stayed at a nearby hotel. Alone in the hotel room I reflected on the past four years. I was amazed by the opportunities I had experienced, and even more grateful for God's presence, provision, and patience.

I also realized that, as the horrendous events of September 11, 2001, unfolded, my greatest fear had not been losing Bruce. I didn't want to lose him, but whatever happened, I had the assurance that he was doing a job he loved. Even more importantly, that he loved God and God was in control.

No, my greatest fear had been for my girls. I didn't want them to blame God for what happened that day—or worse, lose their faith in Him altogether.

But in the hotel room after the ceremony, I thought about the fact that my girls not only still had their faith, but their faith in God was stronger than ever.

And I wept with gratitude.

* * *

"Mom, what would you say if Scott asked your permission to marry me?" Emily asked, as she placed two teacups on the kitchen table.

I stopped pouring the hot water into the teapot, put the kettle down, and turned to her.

"I would ask him if he loved the Lord, his God, with his whole heart, soul, mind, and strength—and if he loved you enough to grow very old with you."

Four years ago, Emily had asked me, "What will happen when I get married?"

Now that question needed an answer.

But we didn't try to answer it right away.

For weeks, we focused on selecting the date, the dress, the bridesmaids, the church, and the location for the reception.

Finally, one day I got brave enough to voice the question I knew we both had been asking ourselves.

"Emily, who do you want to walk you down the aisle?"

"I am going to do that thing you told me about."

"The wedding I saw on TV?"

"Yes, the one where the bride started at the back of the church with no flowers, then had different men who had been father figures in her life hand her flowers as she came down the aisle. And then you can tie all the flowers together with a ribbon."

"Who are you thinking of asking?"

"Definitely Poppy, and I'm still figuring out the others."

She eventually asked my dad (Poppy), her three uncles—James, Arend, and Ken—as well as two friend uncles, Doug and Tony.

We referred to them as the "flower men."

As the date for the wedding approached, we thought better of calling them the flower men in the worship folder. We set out to find a proper term. After investigating various words, we chose *escort*. The true definition of the word *escort* was ideal: one or more persons accompanying another to guide, protect, or show honor.

We included the definition, and a beautiful piece Scott had written, in the worship folder which served a double purpose. It identified the escorts and their significance—and also addressed the elephant in the room.

"In honor of the memory of Bruce Van Hine, the father of the bride, we acknowledge the fact that, while Bruce could never be replaced, God in His grace has provided Emily with men who could stand beside her in love to honor, protect, and guide her in place of where her father would have stood. That is why they stand here today: to, in some small way, point to Love's ability to leak into the cracks and lead us from a brokenness we were never meant to endure toward wholeness."

* * *

Each man stood in the aisle holding two white calla lilies which they gave to Emily as she walked forward. The only thing we hadn't anticipated was they would want to hug her which caused her veil to fall off before she had even made it halfway down the aisle. But it didn't matter.

When Emily reached the front, I tied her flowers with a ribbon, hugged her, and then kissed her on the cheek. It was beautiful, symbolic, and perfect. There wasn't a dry eye in the church.

Any tears I wept that day weren't out of sadness but out of pride for who Emily and Scott were, and gratitude that God had supplied a way when there seemed to be no way. The ceremony and reception were all Emily and Scott hoped it would be.

* * *

That fall, I received information about a volunteer opportunity that piqued my interest. The September 11 Families

Association was looking for docents to share their September 11 stories.

To be honest I had never heard the word docent before, so I looked it up in the dictionary. It means museum guide.

Even though I was apprehensive, I decided to give volunteering a try.

I called to find out more information.

"You need to come in for an interview, and then there is a training session." said Rachel, the docent coordinator.

I wasn't sure if my lack of knowledge about the World Trade Center would be a problem or not. I had only been to the WTC twice in my entire life. Once in my late teens I had taken the PATH train into the WTC, and on July 4, 1976, Bruce and I visited the observation deck of Two WTC with his sister and husband.

I also felt I barely knew anything about September 11, 2001 besides my own story.

What was I thinking?

Actually, I knew exactly what I was thinking. The 9/11 Tribute Center's mission was "person to person" history. I knew I could tell Bruce's and my story. I had done that in churches and at ladies' groups. This was a whole new thing, but I wanted to try.

A few weeks after the interview, I headed back into Lower Manhattan for a two-day training workshop. As I drove to the training, I felt like this could be a mistake.

Lord, I am willing to try this, but I need a sign or something. Please.

As I timidly entered the room, I scanned faces looking for Rachel, the only person I had met before. *Wait! That's Bruce's captain from Squad 41. Someone I know. A nod from God.*

Lee Ielpi, the founder of 9/11 Tribute Center, shared his story and vision. "I'm retired Fire Department. My son Jonathan was killed on 9/11. I had spoken to him early on September 11 as he was heading to his firehouse. Eventually I would head to the site to look for him."

Lee shared about the band of dads—a group of retired firefighters who searched for their firefighter sons—and of finding Jonathan's body in early December 2001. His story was powerful.

Lee went on to state his reason for starting Tribute—to tell the stories. When he had visited the site in recent months, he had noticed many tourists and random people sharing misinformation and incorrect facts about the attacks. He wondered what could happen if the people who had first–hand information had the opportunity to share their perspective. And the 9/11 Tribute Center was born.

The training was proceeding nicely when a staff member mentioned that the volunteers shouldn't get political. *That's not a problem.*

Then a fellow trainee added, "You shouldn't get too religious either." *That could be a problem.*

I thought about the night I spent in the hotel near Meghan's college, when I wept with gratitude at God's protection over my daughters despite all that we had lost.

I thought about Emily's wedding, and how God made ways in all our lives when there appeared to be no way.

I tentatively raised my hand. "If we aren't allowed to mention God, I will respect that, but to tell my story I need to mention God because God is a big part of my story."

Rachel said, "If God is your story, you can mention God."

Another big nod from God.

12

THE POWER OF OUR STORIES

I n March 2006 I began leading tours around the pit that used to be the World Trade Center site.

Twice a month I ventured into Manhattan for tours. I figured out where to park, located the public bathrooms, and found a cafe to purchase coffee. I tried to walk like I belonged.

Inside I was scared to death.

I memorized one route from the parking garage on Murray Street to the starting point of tours at 120 Liberty Street. I didn't deviate from it. Because the Tribute building would be under construction for six more months, the tours started on the street—which is how I ended up approaching total strangers and asking, "Are you here for the tour?"

With normal traffic my commute to the Tribute Center was ninety minutes. Most days it was closer to two hours. Even though it seems wrong to say I *love* doing tours, I do.

I had been extremely anxious about meeting the other docents. Docents fell into one of five categories: family members, downtown residents, survivors, rescue/recovery workers or people who had volunteered with nonprofits, including the Salvation Army and the Red Cross. The media had always referred to family members as either uniformed or civilian—a kind of *us vs them* scenario. I had wondered how civilian family members feel about me as a uniformed family member.

But I'd felt an instant connection with the other Tribute volunteers, a connection that seemed to say *I have a story, you have a story, and we experienced this event differently but together.*

On my tours I began to explain it this way:

"In the beginning I only had my story, which was quite enough, but now I know the stories of survivors, downtown residents, other family members, and rescue/recovery workers. To truly understand September 11, 2001, you have to have *all* those stories. To me they are like a mosaic—a piece of art. They aren't connected like a puzzle. They lay alongside each other to create the picture of what happened."

I realized early on that most of my fellow docents are people I never would've met if we all hadn't volunteered. Those friendships are precious to me.

In addition, while volunteering with 9/11 Tribute Center gave me opportunities to tell Bruce's story, it also allowed me to continue working through my journey—just like therapy.

Soon I discovered additional opportunities for storytelling besides the walking tours. Speaking to groups while sitting on the floor in Gallery Five quickly became a new favorite experience. Sharing with adult groups is rewarding, but my passion is talking to the kiddos.

The youngest students ask the hardest questions.

One group of ten-year-old students sticks in my mind.

"Any questions?" I asked after explaining the timeline and telling my personal story.

Arms waved in the air.

"Yes, young lady, what is your question?"

"Did they arrest the terrorist?"

I paused a moment as I carefully chose my words. *She is trying to understand the inexplicable.*

"Remember when I said the planes crashed into the buildings?" I asked. "So, everyone on the planes died, including the terrorist."

Still more waving arms.

"Yes, sir," I said as I pointed to a young boy.

"But I just don't get it. Why would someone kill themselves as a way to kill someone else?"

"Well, there is a lot of history to be understood but basically they were taught to hate," I said, adding, "And they hated so much that they were willing to die."

The young man hit his palm on his forehead and said, "But I still don't understand."

"I hope you never understand that kind of hate."

I soon discovered that high school students also have questions but don't want to speak up in front of their friends. It didn't take me long to learn to hang around after the presentation for teens who wanted to ask a question or share thoughts.

After speaking to one high school group, I was approached by a young woman wearing a hijab. She told me her father had been arrested and eventually released after the attacks.

I listened and then said, "I'm sorry."

* * *

One day Donna Kaz - a fellow docent, playwright, and activist - invited me to be part of a project called Performing Tribute.

Before I knew it, six of us were sitting around a conference room table recording our stories on Donna's iPhone.

Donna took that recording and wove it into a script for a theatrical reading.

Soon we were performing at the Tribute Center as well as small venues such as churches, libraries, and high schools.

We weren't actors or performers, but that didn't matter. Our tagline described us well: *Ordinary people telling remarkable stories.*

Each time we performed, I ended the reading with these words: "I believe that telling my story makes this real. September 11 is about people, not just numbers and statistics. Telling the stories makes it real. It has to be real for it to matter. And that's why I do this."

After we performed the reading at a Tribute Center fund raiser at the Tribeca Performing Arts Center—a big deal in a big venue—we were reviewed by David Dunlap of the New York Times. I imagined Bruce smiling down and saying, "That's my girl!"

One day I had a telephone interview with a reporter from the *New York Times* that led to one of the most awe-inspiring experiences of my life.

At the end of the interview the reporter asked if he could send a photographer to my house.

A few days later a rather small unassuming man arrived at my home. He asked permission to rearrange some furniture as he set up a couple of shots. His level of enthusiasm was contagious as he gave me direction for the photos: Look over here, smile, etc.

At one point he commented that I had photos of Bruce displayed and stated how as a Buddhist he doesn't display photos of the dead. We had a good conversation about our beliefs and as the conversation continued, he shared about losing his entire family and asked, "Have you seen the movie *The Killing Fields?*"

"No, but I am familiar with the story."

"It is my story."

I was speechless.

Dith Pran was in my living room. He gave me his business card and told me about the work he did speaking to schools.

Wow. Just wow.

A different kind of wow happened sometime later when Jennifer Adams, head of the September 11 Families Association, called to warn me of a story running in the *New York Times* the next day exposing one of my fellow docents as a fraud.

My first reaction was anger. *Wait! What? She made up a story?*

I had only met Tania Head a couple of times, but her story about being dramatically evacuated—while losing her fiancé in the attack—had always been compelling.

On several occasions, Tania had stood next to me as I told my true story—and she told her lies.

As upset as I was about the betrayal, my heart broke for others in the 9/11 community who had befriended her. None of us expected someone to make up a story when we would have gladly traded our stories to not have one.

Not all stories are true. But when the dust settles, believing the best in people is still my preferred mode of operation.

Our lives take different turns, sometimes tragic, sometimes inspiring, sometimes both. And our stories matter.

I know for me, every person who died on September 11 has a story. Telling those stories makes it real. It has to be real for it to matter.

13

A TIME FOR EVERYTHING
UNDER THE SUN

∞

"**H**i, Mom, we're on our way home!"

Meghan and her boyfriend Kyle had picked up Emily and Scott at the airport and were on their way to my house for Christmas celebrations.

The house was decorated and ready, but I wasn't. I thought I would throw up. There was a secret I held close and now needed to share with my girls and their guys. But how?

I sat on the study floor in front of the bookcase and pulled an old Bible off the shelf.

Okay, Lord, what's a good verse I can use to start this conversation?

I flipped through the pages, noticing highlighted verses, but my thoughts were swirling.

"Do not be anxious about anything, but in every situation, by prayer and petition, with thanksgiving, present your requests to God" (Philippians 4:6 NIV).

Please Lord, give me wisdom.

Give me something.

I placed the Bible back on the shelf and checked the time.

They will be here soon. What am I going to say?

I still had no clue.

I thought the most difficult conversation I would ever have with my girls had been when I asked, "Where do you think Daddy is right now?"

But this was harder.

*   *   *

Soon after they arrived, we enjoyed tea and cake. As we were finishing, I said, "I have something important to tell you."

Breathe. You can do this.

Emily reached for Scott's hand.

All eyes were on me.

I made eye contact with no one. "I have breast cancer."

Meghan jumped out of her chair. "No, I can't lose another parent."

I stood and wrapped her in my arms and said, "This isn't September 11. I am not dying. No one is going anywhere."

We sat back down at the table and I briefly shared the journey I had been on for the past month.

"I found a lump months ago, but I didn't want to say anything until I had a prognosis."

Emily asked, "Who else knows?"

"JoEllen and Aunt Christine," I said. "Then I told Pastor Bruce and Auntie Carol. Remember a few weeks ago when the car crashed into the studio? Well, that was the same morning I had my biopsy."

Sometimes truth really is stranger than fiction. JoEllen had taken me for the biopsy on December 6. The biopsy had gone well. Everyone had been kind and reassuring.

Once we got back in the car, I pulled my phone out and found multiple messages and texts from Carol.

"Something must be up," I told JoEllen as I started listening to one of Carol's messages. I couldn't believe what I was hearing!

"Ann, I know this is the morning for your biopsy, but I need to know the name of our insurance company. Someone drove their car through the studio window!"

Apparently, an elderly woman had been driving herself to the beauty parlor next to our studio and, well. . . she ended up visiting us instead.

December 6 had been a memorable day to be sure!

When I mentioned the crash, the kids nodded. I had told them about the incident when it happened but had left out the part about the biopsy—until now.

"What's next?" one of the girls asked.

I told them I had more testing scheduled on Boxing Day—the day after Christmas.

I added, "Emily, you are going back to Seattle with Scott. Meghan, you are still going to Ghana. Once I know the treatment plan, we will figure out your parts. For now, we are going to have a good Christmas."

The next morning over breakfast, Emily gave me the web address for Scott Hamilton's cancer foundation website. Meghan shared that she'd emailed her professor for the Ghana trip who said she would bend the rules and allow Meghan to call home.

"Oh, and Mom, I have one more thing to say," Meghan announced, "I can't shave my head to make you feel better."

Laughter filled the kitchen.

Okay, let's do this!

This was another attack. Another shake–me–to–the–core moment. Followed by another "pile" to sort through and figure out.

It is harder to pray "your will be done" when you are talking about your own life. I knew God could be trusted, but this was not the same as September 11. This felt like I had some control which was almost more disconcerting than having no control.

What if I make the wrong decision? Pick the wrong doctor?

Breast cancer doesn't run in my family. In fact, I was the first person in my family to have any kind of cancer. This was new territory.

Christine had a childhood friend, an oncology nurse, who suggested two questions that would help us decide about doctors:

"Have you seen this kind of cancer before?"

"How often have you treated it?"

JoEllen's brother-in-law had lost his wife to breast cancer just months before my journey began. The day before I was having the port implanted, he spoke words of encouragement and shared what he had learned on the journey. He gave me the kind of road–tested suggestions that only someone who has gone through this kind of experience would know. He even gave me a cancer care kit that included a sleeping cap, satin pillowcase, ginger tea, and peppermints.

He shared hard-won wisdom:

- Never go to the doctor alone.
- Write down your questions.
- Let the doctor know if you decide to take supplements (unfortunately, his wife had taken supplements that counteracted the chemo).

And he kept saying, "You are going to be fine."

I chose to have chemo to shrink the tumor before having surgery. Christine took me to have the port implanted.

On the day of the procedure, a nurse came in to say, "Your pastor is here."

Pastor Bruce had come to pray with me.

I have to admit, it took me several years to call my pastor by his name. It was easier to call him "Pastor" or even just "PB." Speaking the name Bruce for someone other than *my* Bruce was tricky. Eventually, "PB" turned into "Bruce" as my friendship with him and his wife grew.

Chemo was scheduled for every other Friday.

By Monday I would be feeling beat up and would consider it a win to go from the bedroom to the living room couch.

Every day at breakfast, lunch, and dinner a friend called to see if I was okay and if I needed anything. I am pretty sure someone had organized a network of helpers I knew nothing about. Friends would ask if they could grocery shop for me, clean for me, drive me wherever.

Carol and Karen, a former student of ours, would cover my Tuesday classes. On Thursdays, JoEllen drove me to the studio where I taught without leaving my chair. The next week, I would usually feel well enough to drive myself to the studio.

Basically, a bad week was followed by a good week. Repeat.

For every Friday treatment someone went with me, and many times whoever went with me spent the night. Meghan came home from college to take me. Emily flew in from Seattle. Christine drove down from Schenectady, and my local friends lay down their lives to attend to mine. I was so blessed.

I marvel at the women who have to care for families while receiving treatment. I had the luxury of being totally selfish and only thinking about me.

I missed doing tours at the Tribute Center. I continued participating in Performing Tribute but wore a head scarf. I imagine it was probably unnerving for the audience, but I wanted to keep doing what I could. I had a wig, but I decided the head scarf look was more artsy and definitely more "me."

I think losing your hair during chemo is actually a blessing because you don't have the energy to wash or style it anyway. One thing no one tells you about losing your hair is you lose the hair in your nose, so your nose runs constantly. Eventually I had short, dark, curly hair which morphed back into my straight, dirty blonde hair as it grew.

The lumpectomy was scheduled for May about two weeks after chemo ended.

The technician said, "I can't find the lump."

I replied, "That is either chemo or prayer or a combination. I don't care how it happened; I will take it."

Instead of a lumpectomy, my surgeon removed my lymph nodes.

At the follow-up appointment he said, "I have good news and bad news. The good news—no cancer. The bad news—I took all of your lymph nodes."

I was fine with that.

* * *

Three months later, I rented a house on Vancouver Island for a family vacation with my girls and their guys.

Unsure of where I'd be in my recovery, I figured a beautiful spot where I could just sit was a good idea—but I still wanted to be close enough to activities if I felt up to doing them.

Meghan, Kyle, and I flew to Seattle where Emily and Scott joined us. We rode the Victoria Clipper ferry to Vancouver Island.

The house was in an amazing location on its own cove about forty minutes from Victoria.

The first morning we were there, I entered the kitchen and noticed Kyle standing on the deck looking toward the horizon. I walked outside to join him.

"Is that a whale?" he asked as he pointed.

"Wow!"

We both watched in amazement.

After a few moments there was no more evidence of whales, so we went inside for coffee.

"Good morning," I said as Meghan joined us at the kitchen table. "We just saw a few whales."

"Why didn't you wake me?" she asked.

"There wasn't really time," I replied.

"At first we weren't even sure if that was what it was," added Kyle.

The next morning at approximately the same time Meghan came wandering into the kitchen.

I commented, "You're up early."

She replied, "I wanted to see the whales."

"You do know they don't commute."

We laughed.

In pondering the whales, I realized I had to at least be *watching* for whales to stand a chance of seeing them. Kind of like with God. If I'm not looking for evidence of Him, I am not likely to see His fingerprints and handiwork.

On that trip God showed me something else I had never seen before—the end of the rainbow. One morning a rainbow began—or maybe ended—in the cove in front of the house. No pot of gold but wonderful, nonetheless. A special surprise during a fantastic family trip.

* * *

I'd had the summer to start to heal. I began feeling almost like myself. In fact, until I started feeling better, I hadn't realized how bad I'd felt before the surgery. By now it felt like I was on *even* ground instead of climbing out of a hole.

By the end of September, I visited a radiologist to discuss treatment. I quickly learned that radiation is different from chemo in a couple of ways. Chemo treatments can take hours, and you feel bad pretty consistently. Radiation treatments take five minutes, and you feel okay until you don't. The effects come on suddenly and unpredictably.

A friend described the side effects of radiation as a wall you don't want to hit—so you need to learn to take on only about half of what you think you can do.

While leading a Tribute tour, I experienced that learning curve.

The tour was going along fine but as I told my story I started to feel light-headed, and my body felt heavy.

The windowsill of the World Financial Center was a perfect height for me to lean against as I kept talking and acting like all was good.

Only one more stop. I can do this. Please, God, don't let me faint.

As another docent shared her story, I sipped some water and then it was time to move on.

Walking slowly, I led the group to our last stop, which was the Eleven Tears Memorial in the American Express building about two blocks away.

As the tour ended, the other docent said, "Okay, good tour. I'm going to head home from here. Bye." And she left.

I tried not to panic.

Okay, small, slow steps, and I will make it back to Tribute.

My prayer life certainly improved, as with every step I pleaded with God to help me take the next one.

As I reached the South Bridge, I had to stop.

Rest, just rest.

"Ann, are you all right?" It was Meri, the curator from Tribute.

"Actually, no. Can you walk with me?"

"Of course."

When we arrived at Tribute the staff was quite concerned. Questions came in rapid succession.

"Have you eaten today?"

"Should we call an ambulance?"

"Do you need more water?"

"Did you drive in?"

After a phone call to my doctor—and a trip to the firehouse next door for a vitals check, a turkey sandwich, and a bottle of water—I was feeling better but not well enough to drive home.

I called my friend JoEllen, who volunteered to drive with her husband Tim into Manhattan to retrieve me and my car.

After that, I embraced the idea of taking on less, even if I had moments of feeling good.

Lesson learned.

A month later, on my way to my final radiation treatment, the early morning sky had a strange coloring to it. After a few moments I realized it was a rainbow that seemed to start at the treatment center and arch over my entire route.

I thanked God for the visible sign of His promises. Later in the day I emailed family to share my rainbow story and the great news of finally being done with treatments.

Little did I know that just five days later the unimaginable would happen.

As I pulled out of Boston Market with my dinner after a long day of teaching, my cell phone rang.

"Are you driving?" It was Christine.

"Yes."

"I will call you later."

"What's wrong?"

"James is dead."

"What?"

"James is dead."

"What do you mean James is dead?"

I pulled to the side of the road and Christine related the story. Apparently, my brother hadn't shown up for a dental appointment. His wife, Fran, had found him at home, dead on the floor from a pulmonary embolism.

On the list of everything that could happen in life, my little brother dying wasn't on it.

I called Carol, Debbie, and JoEllen for prayer support.

I called Emily and Meghan to tell them the devastating news.

Since my dad had been in a nursing facility after suffering a stroke in September 2006, my mom lived alone. I turned my car around and headed to my childhood home to tell Mom of the death of her only son.

My mom and I packed a few of her things so she could spend the night at my house.

Debbie and JoEllen showed up on my doorstep and we all had a cup of tea and a time of prayer.

"What is the date?" asked my mom.

"It's December 9," I replied.

"Tomorrow is Christine's birthday."

I nodded as I remembered the words from scripture promising that while sorrow lasts for a night, joy comes in the morning.

THE PLAZA

Robert Frost once wrote, "In three words I can sum up everything I've learned about life: it goes on."

And it does. Whatever we face—short of our own death—is not the end.

Eventually we begin to rebuild.

When we've sorted through the pile, and experienced the pit, we start to truly move forward. Some people think you can move on from great loss—but you can't. But you can move forward.

The Plaza begins to take shape.

- The National September 11 Memorial Plaza opened to family members on the tenth anniversary of the attacks. The Plaza opened to the public the next day. Visitors were required to obtain free passes and enter through a security check point onto the Plaza.
- On May 15, 2014 President Barack Obama dedicated the National September 11 Memorial Museum. It officially opened on May 21.
- On May 25, 2014, the fences came down. For the first time since the September 11th attacks, people had open access to the World Trade Center site.

- Construction of the surrounding buildings culminated in three openings, held November 13, 2013, November 3, 2014, and June 2018.
- Liberty Park on the south border of the site was built above the new security screening entrance for all deliveries. In September 2017, the much-disputed Koenig Sphere was placed in Liberty Park.

14

NEW BEGINNINGS
(AND ONE WELL-DESERVED ENDING)

"**M**om, Kyle and I want a small destination wedding," said Meghan as we sat in her apartment drinking our coffee.

"So, are we all flying somewhere?"

"No, in the US, not the beach. Maybe the mountains?"

We decided four hours was a reasonable drive time and drew a circle to narrow the search. Thank God for the internet.

Eventually, Meghan and I took a road trip to Virginia and scoped out a few places. We found the perfect place. A beautiful inn where we could hold the ceremony and reception, and family could stay there as well. The whole place would be ours for the weekend.

The logistics of planning a destination wedding took some doing but with emails, phone calls, and another weekend trip to Virginia with Kyle and his mom, it was coming together. I quickly—and pleasantly—realized that hosting a wedding in Virginia was less expensive than hosting one in New York!

Shortly after we returned from our trip, Pastor Bruce called and asked if he could pass along my contact information to a former member of our church, and I didn't think too much of it. I had known the couple briefly.

I wonder what this is all about.

The mystery was solved on Easter Saturday when Chuck and his wife called to ask if they could drop something off.

They arrived on my doorstep with a small brown package.

Chuck explained that he worked for the company responsible for inscribing names on bronze slabs for the Memorial. He had been working the day they inscribed Bruce's name and filmed the process.

His wife added, "It is like watching grass grow."

As he handed me a DVD and the package, he said, "You can't show this to anyone, or I could lose my job. I thought you would want it. I also saved all the shavings."

His amazing gesture of kindness filled me with gratitude.

For Christmas that year, I filled three glass ornaments with the shavings, added a gold ribbon, and gave one to each of my daughters. I would place the third one on my tree.

On Sunday May 1, 2011, I headed into Manhattan with Debbie to conduct a private tour for her sister, Kathy, and friends.

After the tour, we drove back to Kathy's house for pizza. Heading home around nine that night, I turned the radio on for the first time all day.

I could sense from the tone of the newscasters' voices that something had happened. When I realized what they were talking about, I thought to myself, *I think I should be happy.*

But I felt nothing.

The phone started ringing as I walked in the door. It was Debbie.

"I can't believe we were at the site the day Bin Laden was killed," she said.

"I know. It is weird."

Both of my girls also called. Their reactions were similar to mine: not exactly sure what the "proper" response should be.

Meghan mentioned she thought the timing was interesting with the tenth anniversary only months away. I agreed. Emily wondered if her indifference to Bin Laden's death was because we had always thought of Bruce's death as line of duty. I agreed with that as well.

On Monday morning, I headed into the city for my scheduled Tribute Center tours. I hadn't seen any television reports other than President Obama's announcement from the

White House, so I hadn't seen the images of people celebrating in the streets.

I immediately noticed an increased police presence as I walked the few blocks from the parking garage to the Tribute Center.

The media was everywhere.

It was a zoo.

When I arrived at Tribute Center, Lee Ilepi asked if I wanted to attend the mayor's press conference.

"Whatever you need me to do. Just let me know."

I am not good at recognizing famous or noteworthy people, but at the press conference I recognized Katie Couric.

Oh, my bizarre life, I thought to myself.

After the press conference, I was interviewed by a newspaper reporter who asked, "Can you tell me your reaction to Bin Laden's death?"

"Actually, I'm still processing it."

"So how do you feel?"

"I said I am still processing it."

"It's been ten years, so how does it feel now that Bin Laden is dead?"

"To be honest, I haven't spent the last ten years thinking about Bin Laden. I had two daughters to raise, a small business to run, and a life to lead."

"So how does his death change things for you?"

"The reality is, at the end of May my daughter, Meghan, is getting married, and whether Bin Laden is dead or alive, her dad is not here to walk her down the aisle. Thank you."

In the next few days, so many people reached out to share their thoughts and to ask mine that I felt I had to say something. I wrote a Facebook post that explained my view of the events.

I explained that I see September 11 through two lenses—as an FDNY widow and as a follower of Jesus. Because of those first two lenses, I can't see it through the lens of an ordinary American citizen.

I also shared how my daughters and I always thought of Bruce's death as being in the line of duty and not because of Bin Laden. I expressed my gratitude to our military and my sorrow for the families of those who had been killed in the ongoing struggle against terrorism.

In the following weeks, we wrapped up all the details for Meghan and Kyle's fast-approaching wedding. My mom and I drove to Pennsylvania to pick up some of the items that needed to be transported to Virginia. Kyle's parents had a car full of items as well. Once we arrived, we had a busy time with last minute details at the bakery, florist, and inn.

Thankfully, Saturday dawned as a beautiful day for the outdoor ceremony, with Debbie officiating. Emily descended the long wooden staircase in her bare feet, slipping into her purple heels at the bottom. The staircase was perfect for a dramatic entrance, but Emily's heels were very high and we didn't want *that* dramatic of an entrance.

Meghan descended next, wearing flats and carrying a beautiful floral bouquet into which she had tied Bruce's wedding ring, her way of her daddy walking her down the aisle. Kyle met her at the bottom of the stairs and escorted her to the altar.

During the reception, as maid of honor, Emily shared thoughts that reflected what was in all of our hearts: "Meghan, things haven't turned out the way we thought they would. I'm older, but you are taller. You live in the country, and I live in a city. And Dad isn't here. . . "

After all the festivities were over, I sat on the deck of the inn to enjoy the view with my family all around and gratitude in my heart. As in the past, God's presence, peace, and provision had filled my life and the day.

The thought of hanging up my dancing shoes had been floating around in my head for a while. When I mentioned my thoughts to Carol, she said, "Let's give the business to Jes—then we won't have to clean the studio when we leave."

Jes was one of our teachers, and when we shared our thoughts with her, she was thrilled.

As we began our thirty-fifth season of teaching, Carol and I began easing out of the business, making plans to retire after the recital in June.

We did clean out the storage closet. After so many years, we had accumulated all kinds of treasures: gold sequin hats, red pompoms, silver canes, lots of LPs, and even reel–to–reel tapes. But it was time to say goodbye.

I had no regrets, only amazing memories, and confidence in the future of the studio under Jes's leadership. And Carol was still my best friend even after being my business partner for thirty-five years.

It doesn't get better than that.

15

TEN YEARS AND COUNTING

The joke at Tribute had always been that it wasn't a real
tour unless there was an Australian in the group. And it
was true.

Having a New Yorker on the tour, however, had been rare.
But as the tenth anniversary of the attack drew near, more locals
began visiting the 9/11 Tribute Center.

One couple from Long Island commented, "It's been ten
years. We thought we should come."

By midsummer there were camera crews and reporters
from all over the world. As I walked down the street, I heard
many languages spoken.

On one tour I had a Japanese television crew, a Brazilian
newspaper reporter, twenty tourists, and a Tribute staff member
to help fend off any issues with the media.

For years I had been ending every tour with these words: "Our tour ends here at this beautiful memorial—the American Express Eleven Tears Memorial—but some day there will be a memorial across the street."

That day had finally arrived.

On September 11, 2011— a decade after the attack—eight acres of the World Trade Center site reopened as the National September 11 Memorial Plaza. On that first day, only family members and first responders were permitted. The next day it opened to the general public.

As in the past, I didn't attend the official ceremony at the World Trade Center. To be honest, I don't believe I can take on the collective grief of all of those people.

Near the first anniversary I had mentioned to Emily and Meghan that some anniversaries—the first, fifth, tenth and so on—would get more attention from the media and people in general. As family members we don't need a reminder of how long it has been—we know that every day.

Through the years, depending on each of our schedules, I may or may not be with my daughters on the anniversary. But even when we are apart, we always call each other. We shed a few tears. And I remind Emily and Meghan how much their daddy loved them, and how very proud he would be of the women they have become.

When the memorial opened, I wanted my first visit there to be alone. I ordered my pass through the family–only designated website for the first Monday in October.

It seemed to be a meaningful day to go. Ten years earlier, on the first Monday in October, I had gone back to work for the first time since Bruce's death. We had just held his memorial service and were in the process of establishing our new normal.

There is an expression, "If you want to make God laugh, tell Him your plans." Well, I guess He was chuckling because He had a different idea about my first visit.

On September 26, 2011, I attended a meeting for the Tribute Center Docent Council.

As each of the members arrived, we greeted each other and checked in to see how everyone's September 11 had been.

One thing I have always loved about my fellow docents is our mutual respect of each other's stories. Our September 11 stories—our life stories—are different. But there is a bond we share in wanting to tell our stories and hear other people's stories, as well.

From the eighth floor of 20 Cortlandt Street, the view of the memorial was stunning. The new World Trade Center was taking shape. The memorial had opened. It was exciting to see.

Toward the end of the meeting, Lee stopped by.

"Good to see all of you. Has everyone been to the memorial yet?" he said.

A few people nodded.

"I was there on the eleventh," said Jim, a fellow docent.

"I ordered a ticket for next week," I replied

"Ann, as a family member you can go anytime," said Lee.

"Really, I didn't know that."

At this point the sun was setting and the lights of the memorial came on. The view was breathtaking: the black granite, the white lights, the waterfalls.

Jim commented that he was going to go over to the memorial. Jim had lost his older brother in the attacks. Jim had been there at the opening on September 11, but it was crowded, and he wanted to see it at night.

"Can I go with you?" I asked.

"Of course," he replied.

Before we knew it, the entire Docent Council had decided to join us. We arrived right at 7:30, which was the latest that visitors were allowed to enter. We entered through the family entrance and within moments were through security.

I suddenly realized this was the first time I was walking onto the World Trade Center site since July 4, 1976.

It felt unfamiliar but not unsettling.

It felt like the right time with the right people.

I knew Bruce's name was on panel S13, so we all headed toward the South Pool. As we approached the panel the others stood back.

I approached alone and ran my hand over his name: R. Bruce Van Hine.

I love you. I miss you.

As I watched individual rivulets of the water cascading into the pool before descending via a second waterfall, I thought:

They done good. They listened. Thank you.

As we walked toward the North Pool, I was struck by the fact I had played a part in this. I had a small voice in making this memorial what it was. Memories of attending news conferences and workshops flooded my mind.

I remembered back to May 2003, when Emily and I had attended a public hearing about the design of the 9/11 memorial. At the time, the plan had been for the names to be listed randomly or even alphabetically without differentiating between uniform and civilian deaths.

I had brought one of Bruce's medals to the meeting and stated, "I have a medal from the City of New York that tells me that my husband died in the line of duty. And I would appreciate if this Memorial *says* my husband died in the line of duty."

I had also spoken about keeping the history straight. I said that the names of those who died in Shanksville or at the Pentagon—or during the first terror attack on February 23, 1993 that killed six people—should be listed together along with the location of where they died.

Finally, I'd suggested that if there wasn't a way to distinguish first responders, future generations of children would wonder why no one helped.

Others agreed with me, and our voices mattered. They listened to us.

And now the memorial was here, and I was awed at what God had allowed me to be a part of.

The other thing that struck me as we walked to the North Pool was how strangely wonderful it was that I was here with this group of people, which included a civilian family member, a survivor, a rescue worker, a volunteer, and a downtown resident.

I never would have met these people—who I now count as dear friends—if the attacks of September 11, 2001 hadn't happened.

They had never met Bruce, but they know his story. They didn't have a history with Bruce, but they share life with me.

I did use my pass for the first Monday in October. The memorial is beautiful in the daytime, but it is stunning at night.

* * *

The tenth anniversary brought a renewed interest in all things 9/11.

Donna Kaz secured a grant for *Performing Tribute 9/11*. From late August into early October, we did six performances—four in New York City and two in New Jersey.

Discovery Channel did a live broadcast at American History High School in Newark. The program started with a ten–minute segment of *The Rising*, a documentary that features Lee. I was invited to be part of the panel discussion with Lee, Joe, a fellow docent, Danny Forester, executive producer of the film and Dr. Price, a historian from Rutgers University. Approximately a hundred students were present, and it was televised to 2300 schools around the country. No pressure.

When opportunities similar to this arise, I think, *How am I here? God, I think you have the wrong person.* At times I want to cry because, after all, who am I? Then I remember God's response when Moses asked that very same question: who am I?

God responded, "I will go with you."

God didn't read Moses's resume or state his qualifications. God said, "I will go with you."

So instead, I laugh because only God could bring me to this place.

* * *

The FDNY hosted a service at St Patrick's Cathedral on the tenth anniversary—as they had done on the fifth anniversary. I had attended those events because they felt more manageable to me, even though many people attended.

The services are usually a day or two before September 11. Not being on the actual anniversary is a plus. And to me, the traditions of the FDNY add a safety net. I know what to expect—the sight of hundreds of firefighters from across the nation and around the world parading up Fifth Avenue, the beat of the drums and the bagpipers playing "Amazing Grace."

In one sense the sight of firefighters carrying 343 American flags—one for each firefighter killed on 9/11—rips my heart out. However, it also fills me with pride because one of those flags is for my husband, my firefighter.

It is sad and inspiring at the same time. These services are conducted once every five years.

Once every five years I can do.

*   *   *

For many years the walking tour route went into the air-conditioned World Financial Center.

But when the Memorial opened, the new route kept us primarily outside. That first summer it was hot. During walking tours, I would try to find shade under a leaf, but it didn't work.

That summer, half of the 415 white swamp oak trees that would eventually be planted at the site were in the ground. But they were still small. Eventually more than 400 trees would be planted, growing to 60 feet tall and forming a lush canopy.

I loved the trees from the first time I had seen them.

Back in the fall of 2010 I had heard that the first six trees had been planted and looked forward to seeing them. A few days later, as I turned onto Liberty Street, I spied the trees out of the corner of my eye.

And I had burst into tears.

I had never cried at the site before.

An hour later when a fellow docent pointed out the trees to our tour group, she started crying, too. At least I knew it wasn't just me!

Her explanation of her tears brought clarity to me: she said the trees were the first sign of life on the site since 2001.

That same week I received an email from a filmmaker looking to interview family members about the trees. Scott Elliott had been filming the trees since the inception of the memorial.

His project sounded interesting, so I responded, letting Scott know that Bruce had not only been one of the 343 firefighters killed in the line of duty, but that he had been an arborist on the side. I also let Scott know I volunteered with Tribute.

Scott and I emailed back and forth. He decided he would join one of my tours to see if it was something that might work for the film. Eventually he sought permission from Tribute to film the tour. After the tour he interviewed me.

One day I joked with Scott that my interview would probably end up on the cutting room floor.

He shook his head. "There's no way you'll end up on the cutting room floor. You're the heart of this story."

The Trees, a feature-length documentary, was released at the tenth anniversary. Photos of Bruce as an arborist, shots from my tour, and my reflections about the trees were included.

I have always approached the various opportunities I have been given as chances to tell my story. It is okay if nothing more comes of it.

I just have to do the *part* that is in front of me at that time and leave the rest to whatever God has in mind.

16

JAPAN: FAMILIAR—
BUT NOT REALLY

∞

"**M**om," Emily said excitedly, "most people don't get their once–in–a–lifetime trip twice!"

I had to agree.

In July 2014 I was invited for the second time to join an outreach to Japan sponsored by United States - Japan Foundation, Mount Sinai Hospital, Japan Society, and Tribute Center. The first of these annual outreaches had taken place in 2012.

The outreaches had begun in response to the tremendous suffering caused by the Great East Japan tsunami, earthquake, and nuclear disaster of March 11, 2011. The Tohoku earthquake had triggered the tsunami that had destroyed entire villages and caused the loss of many lives. And miles away, the tsunami caused the meltdown of the reactor at Fukushima nuclear power plant, which led to mass evacuations. Those evacuees still had their homes but due to radiation levels couldn't live there.

The concept of the outreaches was simple: the survivors of 9/11 bringing hope to the survivors of 3/11.

The Tribute Center's connection to Japan went back to 2007 when Japan showed their support by donating 10,000 paper cranes to the newly opened Tribute Center.

The inspiration for the cranes had come from the true story of a twelve–year–old girl who had leukemia due to radiation exposure after the Hiroshima bombing. Shortly before her death in 1955, Sadako set a goal of folding a thousand paper cranes as a way to cope with her illness and share her hope for peace with those around her.

In 2007, among the 10,000 origami cranes donated to the Tribute Center was one red paper crane folded by Sadako and donated by her brother, Masahiro Saski.

After the earthquake in March of 2011, the Tribute Center donated a Sadako–style crane made from World Trade Center steel to Japan. Tribute Center docents, Mount Sinai doctors, and Rotary Club members traveled to Japan to deliver the crane. The Soaring Crane was installed in Kaisezan Park, Koriyama, Fukushima Prefecture. Mounted on a beautiful marble pedestal, the crane was positioned to face toward New York.

During that trip, the docents, doctors, and Rotary Club members visited schools, temporary housing facilities, mental health programs, and other gatherings with a message of support and hope.

It was the first of what would become an annual outreach.

At the time of this writing, I've been invited to go on four of these trips—and counting.

Just traveling to and from Japan from New York is an adventure in itself. First, it's a long flight. You're served not one but *three* meals. There is enough time to watch four complete movies and take a short nap. And when you fly home, with the time change you actually land before you left.

To be honest, the schedule for these trips is grueling. The itineraries are multiple pages long. You get up early, go to bed late in a different hotel just about every night, and travel long hours between appointments, meeting and interacting with many people along the way.

I know five words of Japanese while I am in Japan which I promptly forget when I get home. What I never forget are the people—amazing, gentle, giving people.

On my first visit to Japan, while visiting a storefront mental health center I realized the attendees' faces bore the same expression I'd seen as I glanced in a mirror after September 11. The look of disbelief.

After our presentation, we mingled and chatted with those in attendance.

I struck up a conversation with a twenty–something American guy, who looked a little shell shocked.

"Thank you for sharing your story," he said.

"You're welcome. Are you a student?"

"No, I actually came to Japan as part of a program to teach English."

"That's great. When did you arrive?"

"Late spring of 2011 after the earthquake and tsunami." He added, "I was placed in a school where nearly every student had lost a family member."

"That must have been very difficult," I said. "Actually, I don't think it was fair for you to be put in that situation."

"Well, my time here is coming to a close. I feel bad about leaving when there is still so much to do."

I didn't know what to say.

There was a moment of silence and then I said, "Could you use a mom hug?"

"Yes," he said gratefully. "It has been a long time."

As I hugged him, he burst into tears.

I held him and cried with him.

I felt if my trip to Japan was only to give this kid a mom hug, it was worth it.

One day as we were traveling to our next event, several people's phones sounded with notifications. I looked at my phone and saw in English the words "Emergency Alert."

I started to read on and realized the rest of the message was in Japanese.

So there is an emergency, but what kind?

Just then one of our translators jumped up and said, "Don't worry! It is just an earthquake."

My heart stopped.

Someone else jumped up and quickly explained that it was a small earthquake, and all was well.

One of the best things about these 9/11 to 3/11 trips is that Tribute, Mount Sinai, and Rotary return every year. I think that speaks volumes. Our recurring visits have allowed us to build true friendships and see change not just in the rebuilding, but in the people.

On my first visit, many people were operating on autopilot. They didn't know or trust us, so we did most of the talking. The cultural differences were evident. I observed that the Japanese are a more reserved people than Americans. I also learned that our mental health practices were different.

On my second trip, I saw not only the rebuilding of the infrastructure but the willingness of people to start sharing stories of how their spouses and friends were coping. During my third trip, the people I met shared on a more personal level, speaking about how *they* were doing. By the fourth visit, docent–style programs had started springing up so people could share their stories with a wider audience.

Our tragedies happened a world apart and had different causes—terrorism vs tsunami—but loss is loss. Our team didn't necessarily have answers, but we were further along on the journey of surviving and thriving after a tragedy. We were willing to be present.

My trips to Japan have truly been life–changing opportunities for me. It is hard to believe that Japan was never on my bucket list of places to visit, but today Japan is in my heart. A few things I learned and observed include:

- Being translated is an interesting experience. It makes me choose my words more carefully and even structure my sentences differently.
- Not knowing the language makes me a better listener. It makes me more aware of body language and tone.
- I can read about an event. I can watch videos and see it on the news, but being there and meeting the people makes it real.
- God doesn't waste anything. If I allow Him, He will use my life experiences to encourage others.
- Being present is more important than having answers.

After a presentation in a high school where three students shared their 3/11 stories, I briefly told my story and then said, "I told my daughters, 'September 11 does not define you.' And I want *you* to know that March 11 doesn't define *you*. It will shape you, but it doesn't define you. You have done a great job today telling us your stories. Keep up the good work. I am proud of you."

On the bus to our next stop, one of the Mount Sinai interns commented, "You told your daughters not to let 9/11 define you but everything you do is about 9/11. Wouldn't it be easier to just not deal with it and move on?"

"Good question," I said. "I will have to get back to you with an answer."

It was a thought I had pondered before but hadn't been able to fully process.

Was volunteering at Tribute allowing 9/11 to define me?

I thought on it all evening. The next morning, I had an answer.

September 11 doesn't define me.

I define it.

17

THE STORY CONTINUES

In 2012, I visited the National September 11 Memorial Museum while it was still under construction. The museum had offered Tribute Center docents the opportunity to take a tour.

To me the massive size of the underground museum space alone spoke to the magnitude of the event.

As I descended the stairs down to bedrock, I realized I was looking at the "bathtub walls" I have spoken about on walking tours. They're called "bathtub walls" because, like a bathtub in reverse, they keep the Hudson River out. These seventy–foot walls that were built in the 1960s—and later reinforced with tiebacks—had stood the test of time and attack. I was astonished to see one of the few remaining structures of the original World Trade Center.

Even though at the time the museum was more construction site than galleries, many of the largest artifacts had already been placed inside, including full-size fire trucks and police cars.

In 2014, with the opening of the National Memorial Museum rapidly approaching, I felt an uncomfortable feeling in the pit of my stomach. It is hard to explain but the museum opening was kind of the last piece in the September 11 story. It was a strange, unsettling time.

The recurring thought that kept reverberating in my mind was this: *We cleaned up the site. We provided a memorial. Now the history is ready to be told in the museum, so it is over.*

Once the doors opened it seemed like the story would be set in stone.

But part of me believed the story was still being written. There were still stories to be shared and learned from. I guess John W. Gardner's words sum it up for me: "History never looks like history when you are living through it."

Every single thing connected with the museum—the location, the admission fees, the human remains stored in the medical examiner's office—seemed to cause a media frenzy.

The phrase 9/11 families—as in 9/11 families think this or that—was used and abused. It frustrated me when that phrase was thrown about because it isn't a quote from every single family member or even from a September 11 family spokesperson, since there isn't such a person.

I am fairly confident that most family members don't consider their voice to be a representation for all, but I feel sometimes the media presents it that way. I try to be careful to present my thoughts as *my* thoughts whenever I am interviewed.

The museum opening made me feel uneasy, but the part I wasn't prepared for was on May 14 when the radio newscaster announced, "The fences are down for the first time since September 11, 2001."

For the last eight years, as I led tours around the site and then onto the memorial, there had always been a fence. A fence around an empty hole and then around a construction site. A fence around the memorial that allowed me one point of entry. A fence that kept me out, then kept me safe—and now it was gone.

My mind raced with thoughts.

What if I am on the memorial and some wacko does some wacko thing?

What if I am with a group of children or teens?

Did I have a plan?

And then I remembered what I say to student visitors: "Be aware, not afraid!"

On Thursday, May 15, 2014, President and Mrs. Obama attended the dedication ceremony for the National September 11 Memorial Museum. Stakeholders were selected by lottery to attend. A couple of my fellow docents attended. I did not.

For the first week the museum stayed open twenty-four hours a day to allow family members, 9/11 rescue and recovery workers, survivors, lower Manhattan residents, and first responders from agencies that lost members to view the museum.

I was apprehensive about going, but I wanted to go to see for myself what it was like, so I could comment intelligently if asked about it.

"Do you and Tony want to go to the National September 11 Memorial Museum with me?" I asked Carol. "I'm not really sure if I want to go, but I think I should."

"Sure," replied Carol. "Are Meghan and Kyle coming, too?"

"No, I mentioned it to her, but she wants her first visit to be with just Kyle."

"Tony can drive us in."

"Sounds good," I said. "It will be a short visit if you don't mind. I definitely want to see Bruce's photo, the cross, the Last Column and the Bible, but I am not sure about the rest of it."

"You're the boss." She chuckled.

Docent friends informed me the museum was like visiting the Holocaust Museum. Only problem with that comparison was I had never been to any Holocaust museum or watched Holocaust movies, as that tragedy had always felt overwhelming to me. How much harder would it be to visit a museum where I had a personal connection?

On May 18, Carol, Tony, and I ventured into the museum. As we approached the airport–style security screening to enter the museum, Tony realized his belt had a knife in it. He explained his mistake to the guard as Carol and I looked on and shook our heads in disbelief.

We rode the escalator down to the exhibit halls as I held my breath. I walked quickly through the first dimly lit passageway as I heard recorded voices of people telling where they were as the events unfolded. I walked toward the light I saw ahead of me.

The light at the end was Foundation Hall. I stood on the balcony level surrounded by the bathtub walls as I looked down on a massive open space where the Last Column bearing the letters SQ 41 stood. The vastness and starkness of Foundation Hall seemed to speak to the magnitude of the events.

From there we descended farther down toward the two exhibit areas: In Memoriam and Historical.

"Let's do the in memoriam first," I said as I walked in that direction.

As we entered the dimly lit space, we noticed the walls covered with the photos of all the people killed on September 11 as well as the six victims of February 26, 1993.

We quickly realized the photos/names were alphabetical and walked in the direction of the end of the alphabet toward the Vs. Bruce's photo was at the bottom of a row.

We glanced in the display cases to see personal items that families had donated, including sports jerseys and a flute. I had donated Bruce's Appalachian Trail maps which weren't on display yet but would be a year later.

Carol, Tony, and I walked over to video tables. I searched Bruce's name. We viewed the photos I had donated—Meghan and Bruce at her eighth–grade graduation, Bruce and Charlie on the Appalachian Trail.

I lifted one of the handsets, placed it to my ear, and heard my own voice:

"Bruce left Bibles on the Appalachian trail. . . "

Future family members will hear my voice telling stories of Bruce. That's cool.

I cautiously entered the historical area of the museum through a revolving doorway.

I wasn't sure how much I wanted to see. I didn't stop to watch or read most of what was displayed. I sought out what I thought were safe images.

I was particularly fascinated by an animated video showing the contrails of commercial jets traveling through the sky becoming fewer and fewer as US airspace closed. I stood and watched that a few times.

I realized on the wall there was a double timeline showing what was happening in the air in parallel with what was happening on the ground. It provided an interesting perspective.

As I turned the corner to enter the next area, I heard the voice message Brian Sweeney had left for his wife.

I turned to Carol and said, "I know her."

In that moment I understood that the museum was more than history or even current events. It was the lives of my friends laid bare before the world. It was personal.

We continued to check off my list of items. The cross was a little difficult to locate in the museum, but we found it. Early on during the rescue efforts a steel worker found two pieces of steel in the shape of a cross. The steel was removed from the pile and placed on a cement pedestal. Those pieces of steel became known as the Ground Zero Cross and brought hope and encouragement to many.

I had first seen it when it had stood on the corner of Liberty and Church Street at the edge of the Pit.

There was some controversy about the cross being placed in the National September 11 Museum. The courts decided that the cross didn't promote Christianity, but it had been a symbol of hope and could be placed in the museum. In my mind it is the ultimate symbol of hope—the hope of salvation. I was glad to see it placed in the museum.

Next on my list was the Bible that was found in the rubble. The Bible didn't look like a book anymore. In fact, it was simply a piece paper that was melted onto a piece of steel. The page that was visible was Matthew 5. "Ye have heard that it hath been said, An eye for an eye, and a tooth for a tooth: But I say, That ye resist not evil: but whoever shall smite thee on thy right cheek, turn to him the other also."

There were unexpected items that broadened my understanding, like the video taken from the International Space Station. NASA Astronaut Frank Culbertson and two Russian cosmonauts were circling the earth on September 11, 2001. After being informed of the attacks, Commander Culbertson had set up cameras to record the event.

He said, "New Yorkers, your city still looks good from space. . . Our country still looks good."

I can't imagine what it must have been like to be in space as your country is attacked.

The gallery about the World Trade Center before the attacks provided a refreshing break from the destruction of September 11, 2001. I kept my eyes straight ahead and basically ran through the gallery on terrorism. Couldn't do it.

The Last Column in Foundation Hall was the final thing on my list of things to see.

I had saved it to the end for a reason.

On May 28, 2002, during a ceremony to close the site, the Last Column had been carried out in similar fashion to the way bodies had been carried out: up the ramp and covered with an American flag. The column of steel bore, in spray paint, the letters and numbers FDNY 343, NYPD 23, PAPD 37.

The letters SQ41 had also been painted on the column.

What I didn't know until 2014 was that SQ41 had been the first thing painted on that column. Squad 41 firefighters had sprayed SQ41 on the steel column as it stood in the pile of debris to mark the area they found Bruce's body.

As we rode the escalator up to the plaza level, "Amazing Grace" blared in the background. I said to Carol, "Wow, like we needed something else. Just rip my heart out and stomp on it."

Walking to the parking garage I thanked Carol and Tony for coming. "I needed to do this with you because I knew I couldn't take care of anyone today and if need be, you would've taken care of me."

I truly believe the museum will teach the next generation about September 11, 2001. My struggle is how much of it do those who lived it need to see. So, I tell everyone to be kind to yourself.

The opening of the National Museum offered a new opportunity to share my story through a joint program with the 9/11 Tribute Center called *We Were There*. Two Tribute Center docents share our stories in the small auditorium in the museum.

The first time I participated in *We Were There* was with Scott Scrimpe, a Squad 41 firefighter. He finished his story by saying, "We promised the wives we would bring home their husbands."

Then I stood up to speak and began my story by saying, "I am one of those wives."

It seems wrong to say I enjoy telling my story. I guess a better way to say it is I appreciate the opportunity to tell my story. It is a satisfying experience. As a friend and fellow docent says, "Telling our stories does more for us the tellers than you the listener."

Some of my fellow docents decided to develop our friendships outside of the time we spent volunteering together. I was excited to be included. The TLA—Tribute Ladies Auxiliary, as we call ourselves—was born. Michele, a fellow docent, took the idea of "Let's be tourists in our own city" and ran with it. She researched and scheduled events.

Every other month or so we participate in the kind of activity—walking tour, museum, or landmark visit—that tourists enjoy. We explore our own city. We've taken tours of Madison Square Garden, the Waldorf Astoria, Brooklyn Navy Yard, and Radio City to name just a few. A meal together is usually part of our adventures. The added time together has expanded our knowledge of our city immeasurably and, even better, grown our friendships. I cherish each one of these bonds.

One of these friendships came as a complete surprise.

If you had told me years ago that Brenda Berkman and I would be friends, I would've found that hard to believe.

As a 9/11 first responder, Brenda was a fellow docent at the Tribute Museum. I knew of Brenda because she was the first female firefighter in the FDNY. Her lawsuit against the city caused a hiring delay that resulted in Bruce waiting years to become a firefighter. At the time all I saw was a roadblock to my husband's dream. What I understand now is that an amazing human being fought for the rights of women to be firefighters not by lowering the standards but by making the requirements fit the job.

When Brenda and I met as docents, I knew who she was, and she knew I was Bruce's widow. As I came to know her as a person, I knew I had to say something.

I eventually said to her, "You know at one point you were a swear word in my house. Now you are a friend."

Amazing what getting to know someone can accomplish.

18

LOST AND FOUND

∞

A Facebook message from a K9 handler brought a delightful Father's Day surprise in 2014.

Unbeknownst to me, the TSA K9 program had been naming dogs after the American heroes who sacrificed their lives on September 11, 2001.

So when a state trooper messaged me and said he was now the handler for Van Hine, I was surprised and delighted.

Bruce would have loved that.

Van Hine was a three–year–old yellow lab trained as a narcotics dog for the TSA and then adopted by the Texas state police. His new handler wanted to let me know how honored he was to work with Van Hine. He sent me photos, and Meghan sent him Squad 41 t-shirts.

A lovely friendship developed. A few years later when we visited his home state, he supplied great information on restaurants and sights to see. Unfortunately, we were still too far away to meet.

Recently, Ryan received a promotion and tried to personally adopt Van Hine, but Van Hine is too good at his job, so the adoption was denied. Van Hine is still fighting crime and Ryan has an open invitation from me for a free walking tour.

Thankfully, understanding the workings of the stock exchange was not a prerequisite for ringing the bell at Nasdaq as a representative of the 9/11 Tribute Center. I was invited to do so on one of the anniversaries of 9/11. It was another one of those running–with–the–big–kids opportunities God gave me. As I often did, I wondered if God had me confused with someone else.

On this particular September 11, I was joined at the Nasdaq stock exchange in Times Square by representatives of the FDNY, NYPD, and Tuesday's Children. We each signed our names on the screen and then hit the button—aka bell—at 9:30 to start the trading session.

Afterwards, we proceeded outside for official photos. During the photo shoot, the Nasdaq staff person told me to turn around. Behind me was the giant Nasdaq sign—*NASDAQ welcomes Ann Van Hine.*

I laughed.

My dream for many years had been to dance on Broadway. Miss Betty, my dance teacher, frequently said, "Stick with me, kid. You will have your name in lights and your backside in tights."

Dance hadn't gotten me here. Bruce had. More correctly, God had.

Days later, when the photos arrived, I saw that my feet were in first position.

I chuckled to myself.

At the end of January, I received a phone call from a Tribute staff member asking if I was available to travel to Brussels in March to speak at a hearing on terrorism at the European Parliament. Lee Ielpi wasn't available, and they wanted me to go instead.

I looked at my calendar. "I am speaking at the Asia Society event on March 8."

"Don't worry, you will be back in time."

Being back in time was the least of my worries.

My good friends, Doug and Rene, have joked that the phrase "speaking at the European Parliament" and my name don't belong in the same sentence. I totally agree. But that is what happened.

The European Peoples Party (EPP) Group held a public hearing on Victims of Terrorism hosted by Teresa Jimenez-Becerril Barrio, a Spanish politician, and I was a panelist. Talk about surprises!

This was definitely a time I said, "Who am I to be invited to speak at the European Parliament?"

God said, "I will be with you."

And He was.

Since I was traveling to Brussels alone, I did my research. How much should a taxi from the airport cost? How do I get from the airport to the hotel?

Ms. Barrio's office was helpful in answering questions and reserving a hotel.

On the day of the hearing, a staff member met me at the hotel, and we walked over to the European Parliament Building. The hearings focused on the need for the European Parliament to have a plan for supporting victims in the event of a terrorist attack.

I was the only American at the hearing. I felt like I was representing not only the Tribute Museum and 9/11 families, but the whole of the United States.

No pressure.

In March 2016, American politics was a hot topic for discussion. President Trump was then candidate Trump, and the people I met found American politics to be "so entertaining."

At the hearing, I told my September 11 story with emphasis on my support systems—the FDNY, my church, my friends, and my daughters' school community.

I mentioned I had chosen to not participate in the Victim Compensation Fund available through the US government as that required giving up the right to sue the airlines. Giving up my rights even though I would probably never sue the airline wasn't something I was willing to do.

I ended my speech by saying, "The FDNY had a plan for line-of-duty deaths. That plan was tested to the limits after September 11 due to the large number of firefighters killed. I encourage you to have a plan that hopefully will never have to be used, although in today's world that is probably not the case."

Unfortunately, three weeks later there was a terrorist attack in Brussels, right where I had been. It was all too real. I had walked those streets.

I reached out to those I had met and let them know I was praying for them. Thankfully, the people I had met and their families were safe.

September 11, 2016 was a Sunday, and I was invited to speak at Resurrection Church of the Nazarene in Manhattan. It was the first time I had spoken in NYC on September 11.

In thinking about speaking to people who had been in the vicinity of the attack on September 11, 2001—people who had witnessed and experienced it firsthand—I wrote the following:

REMOVED

I haven't walked down the stairs in the shoes of the businessperson fleeing the building.

I haven't climbed up the stairs in the boots of the firefighters arriving to rescue and aid.

I haven't run away in my bare feet toward the Hudson to find safety.

I haven't stood in my black uniform shoes, directing thousands to safety.

I haven't knelt on the ground to treat the injured.

I haven't said a prayer over a dead body.

I haven't dived under a car or into a building to seek safety.

In one way I was removed from September 11, 2001; I wasn't there.

And then. . .

I walked in the shoes of an FDNY widow.

I walked in the shoes of a 9/11 Tribute Center docent.

I walked in the shoes of a keeper of the story.

Speaking at Resurrection Church was a unique opportunity as the church is housed in the basement of an Episcopal Church. A few days before, I learned the two congregations had decided to join together for service on September 11. I spoke to both congregations. I grew up in the Episcopal Church and for the past thirty-five years attended Church of the Nazarene, so it was a joining of my faith traditions. It felt like home.

Through the Tribute Museum, a *Wall Street Journal* reporter interviewed me and published two different stories for the fifteenth anniversary.

It was supposed to be one story. I guess I talked too much.

In my defense she came on a tour *and* interviewed me, so I guess she had a lot of information. The one article, "A 9/11 Story: Helping a Husband Follow His Dream of Becoming a Firefighter," was a beautiful telling of Bruce's and my story.

The other article, "For 9/11 Widow 'Life Came Back,'" is a profile piece and includes information on Tribute.

Both articles were published in the same issue of the *Wall Street Journal*.

I read about a new Broadway show called *Come From Away*. I was aware of the basic story: thirty-eight planes flying to America from Europe on September 11, 2001 were forced to land in Canada due to the emergency closing of American airspace.

I was a little skeptical of a Broadway musical about September 11. Nothing about that seemed to go together. However, I wanted to be able to comment intelligently when people asked me about it (which they undoubtedly would), so I suggested to Michele that the Tribute Ladies group should see it. We bought tickets.

Then I, as a 9/11 FDNY family member, received an invitation to see a dress rehearsal so I called Carol to ask her to join me.

The set was visible as we entered the theater. There was no curtain hiding the stage, sparsely decorated with a few chairs, tables, and trees.

Okay, this should be interesting.

The performance began, and I was immediately drawn in by the upbeat music and fast–paced storyline. One moment I was laughing and the next searching for a tissue to wipe away tears only to be chuckling a few moments later.

A cast of twelve actors transformed into different characters by simply adopting an accent or adding a hat, scarf, or jacket.

Many times, I have commented that the stories of September 11, 2001, are like a mosaic. The stories don't fit together like a puzzle. Instead, they lay next to each other to form the larger narrative of what happened that day and since.

As I watched *Come from Away*, my eyes were opened to yet another account of September 11. The people on the rerouted planes had no idea what was happening. Most didn't speak English and were totally in the dark. I can't imagine that level of uncertainty and fear. Yes, I experienced fear and uncertainty, but I was home with my family and friends.

In one of the scenes, people listened to the American president address the nation. *I didn't know the president addressed the nation. I never heard that.*

I remember thinking, *Their story is so different from mine.*

But at that moment there was scene that tied us together: The passengers were being placed on school buses to be driven to schools, Elks Clubs, Salvation Army Camp for shelter.

Realizing how frightened his passengers were, one of the bus drivers noticed a woman holding a Bible.

He knew she didn't speak English but also realized her Bible would be set up the same way as his Bible. Gently taking the book from her, he flipped through the pages until he found Philippians 4:6: *"Do not be anxious about anything, but in everything, by prayer and petition, with thanksgiving, present your requests to God."*

As he pointed to the words, the woman smiled.

In the play, the bus driver explained, "And that is how we started speaking the same language."

And that is when I started crying.

Philippians 4:6 was the same verse that had comforted me.

One of the last lines of the show is this:

"Tonight we honor what was lost, but we commemorate what we found."

Bingo! That's it!

Those words perfectly sum up my life over the last sixteen years.

I have tried to honor Bruce and his sacrifice, but what I have found is worth commemorating, too.

To quote one of my Tribute friends, *"Come From Away* is the essence of our story. . . our group had a storyline similar to the play, in that there was shock, suffering, dealing with the trauma, but finding our way to healing through each other. . . I am sad that this is the way we came together, but my life is richer with the addition of these relationships. We did indeed find each other."

I couldn't have said it better myself.

As I embarked on a journey I never expected or wanted, the choice to rest in my Heavenly Father's arms was the right one. That doesn't mean I haven't looked at the ceiling when the hot water heater flooded, or looked up at the sky when the car won't start, and yelled, "Are you kidding me?"

I'm still not sure if the comment is directed toward God or Bruce.

Perhaps it doesn't matter. God is big enough to handle my questions. And I like to think on occasion Bruce looks down and says, "That's my girl."

In one way I can say the past sixteen years has been nothing but surprises. But in another way, there have been no surprises. God was/is who the Bible says He is. He was/is faithful even when I am not. He has never left me or forsaken me. He has gone with me and before me.

The brotherhood of the fire department has been true to their commitment to care for their fallen members' families. The FDNY and Greenwood Lake Volunteer Fire Department have been true to their promises.

My friends and family have stood by me and walked with me on this journey of navigating something so much bigger than our story.

I am still not big on surprises, but I am learning to go with the flow and trust that God has it all under control; trust that He is never surprised.

God also doesn't waste anything.

All that I have been through He will use for His glory. I just have to trust Him.

AFTERWORD

∞

The memorial was busy with a gentle buzz of activity. I noticed faces of visitors from many nations, heard softly spoken words, saw tears wiped from cheeks and selfies snapped, and listened to the sound of the south waterfall.

As we headed back to the 9/11 Tribute Museum, Stephen, a gentleman in every sense of the word, carried the bag containing the audio headsets. On this walking tour, I was the lead docent and Stephen was my support person. A FDNY firefighter, he was new to the program and a little apprehensive—but when he spoke of *his guys* you heard and saw his passion, his expertise.

As we walked along, Stephen said, "We never called it Ground Zero."

We stopped walking.

Stephen continued. "We called it the Pile and as it got lower, we called it the Pit."

The Pile I had seen for myself on September 28, 2001. I remembered the Pit as a massive hole in the ground when

I had started volunteering at the 9/11 Tribute Center in 2006.

We continued walking and I said, "And now it is the Plaza."

He nodded in agreement.

Our conversation confirmed in my mind something I had pondered for a while. This place and I had been on parallel journeys. We had weathered the attacks, sorted through the debris (the Pile), filled the void (the Pit) and remembered and honored those we lost as we journeyed forward (the Plaza).

The World Trade Center and I had become travel companions.

AUTHOR'S NOTE

As the twentieth anniversary of the attacks approaches, the world is still dealing with a global pandemic. The earliest draft of this memoir was completed in 2017 and even though a pandemic wasn't on my radar the truths from this book can apply.

- The pandemic doesn't define us. We define it.
- We weren't all in the same boat during this crazy time. We weren't necessarily even in the same storm. But we were each in a storm.
- Just as we need all the stories to understand September 11, the same is true of the pandemic. I believe all our stories form a mosaic. They aren't necessarily interconnected like a puzzle but lay alongside each other to create the picture of what happened, a living snapshot of what we went through.

BRUCE'S DAY

∞

Before Bruce had even headed to work on Sunday September 9, 2001, we had decided he would spend Monday night at the firehouse. After all, why drive all the way back home when he was working a day tour on Tuesday September 11?

On Monday evening, September 10, Bruce had called home to see how his girls were doing. That conversation was so ordinary that I remember none of it. I most likely ended that call with the words "I love you," as was my habit.

What I know of his experiences on September 11 has been pieced together from speaking with firefighters from Squad 41. An early call had come into the firehouse before the 9:00 am shift change. Bruce had volunteered to go on that run so the firefighter he was relieving could leave a little early.

As Squad 41 had been returning to quarters, the first plane hit 1 WTC, the North Tower.

The men were redirected to Squad 18 in Manhattan.

The second plane hitting 2 WTC, the South Tower, rerouted the firefighters again, this time straight to the World Trade Center site.

They entered 2 WTC, began climbing the stairs, came across injured civilians, and began escorting them from the building.

Bruce was probably on the first sky lobby when the building collapsed.

I didn't know any of this until his body was found in March 2002.

But some things I had known for years: Bruce was a well–trained member of the FDNY, he was living his dream, and he was willing to lay down his life to save others. We both had accepted that death was a possibility. I understood that his decision to go into the building on September 11 was made long before that day arrived.

When Bruce received the news in March 1990 that he'd been appointed to the FDNY, he wrote me this letter:

"Dear Ann, I never thought that this day would ever happen. In 1973 in California, I read Report from Engine Co. 82. Those people in the book seemed out of reach. Never did I dream that I would be a NYC firefighter. I never thought I had what it took to be a firefighter in the Big Apple. This could not have been possible without your encouragement and love. I thank the Lord for you and this day. I'll always love you."

Signed *Bruce*.

He added one more thought.

"See you later."

RELEVANT LINKS

∞

www.911tribute.org

9/11 Tribute Museum

92 Greenwich St, New York, New York 10006

Offers walking tours led by survivors, first responders, family members, downtown residents, and recovery volunteers. You can schedule online. Also, a small museum that focuses on the stories of those affected by the attacks. There is an admission fee and charge for walking tour. A good starting point. If you have children, this is the place to introduce them to the history and stories. This is who I volunteer with.

www.911memorial.org

National September 11th Memorial and Museum

180 Greenwich St, New York, New York 10007

The memorial is free. I would recommend for children.

The museum is a paid timed admission museum. The museum is large you should plan to be there for at least two hours. I don't recommend it for children.

www.pentagonmemorial.org
Pentagon Memorial
1 N Rotary Rd, Arlington, VA 22202
Outdoor memorial. Admission is free. I would recommend for children.

www.nps.gov
Flight 93 National Memorial
6424 Lincoln Highway, Stoystown, PA 15563
Outdoor memorial and visitor center. Part of the National Park Service. No entrance fees. I would recommend outdoor memorial for children.

www.911trail.org
September 11 National Memorial Trail
Trailheads throughout the East Coast
This is a 1300–mile multi–use trail connecting the three sites of the September 11 attacks.

ABOUT THE AUTHOR

Ann Clark Van Hine, aka Miss Ann, was born in Oxford, England but grew up in Oklahoma, Utah, Arizona, and New Jersey. Today she lives in Brooklyn, New York. Ann is the mom of two grown daughters, the widow of an FDNY firefighter, a retired small business owner, a docent with the 9/11 Tribute Museum, published writer, children's ministries volunteer, and a breast cancer survivor.

Since September 11, 2001, Ann has had numerous opportunities to share the story of God's presence and peace as she navigated "a personal loss in the midst of a national tragedy." She has shared her story all over the USA and internationally in Ireland, Belgium, England, and Japan. Ann is available to speak. To learn more, visit: www.annvanhine.com

CPSIA information can be obtained
at www.ICGtesting.com
Printed in the USA
BVHW031802120821
614283BV00002B/320